# THE Life GOD BLESSES

## Weathering the Storms of Life That Threaten the Soul

### GORDON MacDONALD

**THOMAS NELSON PUBLISHERS**
Nashville • Atlanta • London • Vancouver

Published in Nashville, Tennessee, by Thomas Nelson, Inc.

The Bible version used in this publication is THE NEW KING JAMES VERSION. Copyright © 1979, 1980, 1982, Thomas Nelson, Inc., Publishers.

Scripture quotations noted NASB are from the NEW AMERICAN STANDARD BIBLE®, Copyright © The Lockman Foundation 1960, 1962, 1963, 1968, 1971, 1972, 1973, 1975, 1977. Used by permission.

Scripture quotations noted PHILLIPS are from J. B. Phillips: THE NEW TESTAMENT IN MODERN ENGLISH, Revised Edition. © J. B. Phillips 1958, 1960, 1972. Used by permission of Macmillan Publishing Co., Inc.

Scripture quotations marked NIV are taken from the HOLY BIBLE: NEW INTERNATIONAL VERSION®, © 1973, 1978, 1984 by the International Bible Society, used by permission of Zondervan Publishing House. All rights reserved.

Library of Congress Cataloging-in-Publication Data

MacDonald, Gordon.
    The life God blesses / Gordon MacDonald.
      p.  cm.—(The Gordon MacDonald bestseller series)
    Originally published: Nashville : T. Nelson, c1994.
    Includes bibliographical references.
    ISBN 0-7852-7160-0 (pbk.)
    1. Christian life.  I. Title.  II. Series.
  [BV4501.2.M2267   1997]
  248.4—dc21                                   97–6538
                                                      CIP

Printed in the United States of America.

11 12 — 04 03 02 01

# THE Life GOD BLESSES

Books by Gordon MacDonald
from Thomas Nelson Publishers

*Christ Followers in the Real World*
*The Life God Blesses*
*Ordering Your Private World*
*Rebuilding Your Broken World*
*Renewing Your Spiritual Passion*
*When Men Think Private Thoughts*

# IN
# GRATITUDE

To Gail,
my wife, who walked through each page of this
book, who encouraged me in its writing, and
who lives fully the ideals set forth on
every page. She is the one with the most
beautiful soul.

To Victor Oliver,
my long-suffering publisher, who has been there
from the first day I began to write books.

And to a number of the finest friends
a man could have, who prayed me through this
process and continually reminded me that they
believed in me.

# CONTENTS

# THE LIFE GOD BLESSES

THE GOD OF the Bible blesses lives. Meaning that He stands willing—in fact, desires—to pour out upon people gracious and uncommon gifts. Gifts that might include personal affirmation, intimate relationship, extraordinary challenges to destiny, and remarkable energies that surpass the limits of what we think of as normal human experience. These gifts that enlarge the human experience are things we often desire and seek. But perhaps not always at the correct source or for the right reasons.

God has been blessing lives since the great Beginning. He has done it in so many different ways, to so many different people, and at so many different times and places that one would be a fool to claim to be able to understand the whole process or to reduce it to a simple formula. Occasionally you enter the orbit of someone who likes to convey the impression of having the exclusive word on the subject of how and why God blesses a certain nation, a certain religious tradition, a certain theology, or a certain individual. But such "exclusive words" never stand the test of time. God will not suffer the parochial and self-aggrandizing descriptions and definitions of fools.

Not wanting to be such a fool, I have struggled with grave

doubts that I had even a first word (let alone a last one) to offer on the subject of blessing and the issues behind it. God's *blessing*—and what it involves—is so vast, so humbling, so unpredictable a topic. Yet such a real one.

As I engaged the subject of the life God blesses in the earliest of my writing days, the obvious was quick to assert itself upon me: that the Bible is a compendium—a virtual ancient Who's Who—of lives God has blessed. Different—very different—kinds of people: men and women, older and younger, calm and retiring or feisty and aggressive. People from varying generations over many centuries, distinct from one another to such a degree that they might not have gotten along very well had they shared the same playing field.

If you like using your imagination, select some obviously blessed people and match them together. For example, try pairing up Joshua the MacArthur-like general with Timothy the gentle, somewhat introverted pastor. Or tough and calculating Esther with reflective and responsive Mary, Jesus' mother. How about rough-and-ready Simon Peter with the calm and brilliant Daniel? Think these folks would have done, said, or seen most things the same way? Think they would have easily gotten along? They're blessed people, mind you, but on the surface of things where personality, talent, and temperament are important matters, these are very, very different folks. There are some of them I'd love to take to lunch; there are others I wouldn't want to have my phone number.

Where to begin when one inquires of the life God blesses? What does it mean to be blessed? And what is behind the act of blessing? *And* what must I do to invite the blessing of God?

Is there a sense in which any of us can say, "I have a life God has blessed at one time or another"? My first reaction is an emphatic yes.

For example, if blessing means, first of all, receiving the love of God, then I have a life God blesses. And if blessing means receiving the mercy and restorative grace of God, then I have a life

God has blessed. If I have a life that has occasionally experienced unusual empowerment, a moment in which there is a lifting above normal limits of wisdom and strength, then I have a life God has blessed. And if, in a period of solitude, there has been an unforgettable sense of insight, an indescribable awareness of closeness with the divine, a sudden feeling of liberation to praise and worship, then I have a life God has blessed.

Furthermore, if there is ever a moment when a dream captures one's spirit, a dream to serve or add value to the lives of others, then I have a life God has blessed. Another thought: if a person has found himself in a relationship where there is a quality of human connection that is more enduring and satisfying than what is merely sexual, contractual, or emotional, then he or she has a life God has blessed.

But having said even this, I feel as if I have barely moved the topsoil away from an awesome thought, often underestimated, often taken for granted. The experience of being blessed! *That event(s) in which the Lord God, Creator of the heavens and earth, establishes an intimacy with a man or a woman and draws the person closer to that quality and capacity of humanity originally intended when the first man and the first woman were created. That event in which one may be endowed with unusual powers to be an envoy for the kingdom of God.*

Now, if we talk about lives God blesses, then or now, we're headed for trouble if we stay at the surface of personality and activity. Blessing rarely seems tied to things that are visible. Remain there, and I'm not sure we'll learn a thing that will be helpful.

So this is the point. If there are universals or commonalities in these ancient men and women God blessed, and if there are connectors between them and us, you'll probably find them only in the interior sectors of life—the deeper part of every one of us that no one but God can see with the eye, hear with the ear, or touch with the hand. The deeper levels of who we are. Soul-level.

Descend to the deeper levels of a person—if you can—and

you begin to discover some shared characteristics among this disparate group of biblical people I mentioned. Similarities that transcend the generations, the cultures, the genders, the temperaments. There, at soul-level, is where one might begin to find the keys to the life God blesses.

If you want to think through the subject of the life God blesses, go then to the soul, to the deepest parts of "inner space" where God is most likely to visit with a person, whisper His secrets, establish convictions, heal spiritual wounds, generate hope and courage. If there is something to this business of being blessed by God, that's where you'll find the answers. Nowhere else.

If we are to discuss the "blessable" life, we will have to understand that we're talking about a life lived—are you really ready for this phrase?—*out of the soul.*

The soul is the deeper part of all of us that others cannot see. It is the quiet part where people are most apt to connect with God. In that deeper, quiet piece of spiritual geography there was, in biblical times, and is today, dialogue with heaven, events of repentance, praise, and worship, and the formation of intentions to life and knowledge that enable people to become what I like to call kingdom-builders.

In the Gospels, Jesus uses the word *soul* quite frequently. When He does, He seems to interchange it with another biblical word, the *heart.* St. Paul is not afraid of the word *soul* but seems to prefer *heart* when he speaks of matters interior to humanity. Neither one is reluctant to mean the same thing by using the word *spirit.*

My sense is that a large part of our Western world knows or cares little about this inner part that is called the soul, the spirit, or the heart. The New Age Movement—an amorphous, hard-to-define group—is indeed an exception. If New Agers have anything in common, it is that they are very much aware of the interiority of humanity. The New Ager loves the word *soul* and uses it frequently, if not accurately. In fact, the New Ager has so powerfully grabbed on to the word and the concept behind it that some Christians (not thinking too clearly, I believe) have become skittish about using it. I find myself a bit incredulous when someone comes up after a talk I've given and questions my use of the word *soul*. "Aren't you dabbling in New Age thought when you talk about the soul?" the person asks.

In the non–New Age world, modern people prefer to laud the mind and listen to the emotions. But certainly not the soul! Most of them are in denial about such spiritual inner space. It's strange territory to them. Only when contemporary events become scary, out of control, do such folk cast a momentary glance in the direction of the soul or, for that matter, the holy person who lives life out of that soul.

A biblical case in point: I've always been fascinated by the abrupt action of the Older Testament Zedekiah, king of Jerusalem, who, when his world was falling apart, sent a message to Jeremiah the prophet saying, "Please pray for us." Then later, when Jeremiah was arrested, he summoned him into the royal presence and pleaded the answer to this question: "Is there a word from God?"

Those are soul-oriented comments and questions, and they suggest that Zedekiah was smart enough to know that when all else fails, you turn to men and women who have spent time developing the "muscles" of the soul.

The issue, then, of what kind of a life God blesses is a soul-oriented one: what it means to live out of this soul.

So why tackle a book with the title *The Life God Blesses* and suggest that it all has to do with the state of a person's soul and how he or she lives out of it?

Well, in case someone has not noticed, we appear to have a mass of people of inestimable size in religion who are awakening to the fact their faith isn't working. Or put it this way: they have no sense that God has blessed their lives. Rather than feel blessed, they feel let down, disappointed, and deflated. What seems to have been effective for others isn't for them.

I can witness to this experience. I knew it well as a younger man. And I have known it occasionally as an older one. Times when things flew out of focus, when faith became only empty words, when you couldn't tell the difference between emotion and spirit, a pure motive and a tainted one. In the early days of my faith journey, I did a lot of pretending. I felt suffocated by perceived expectations of a kind of religious or spiritual performance: right responses, right answers, right words, right deeds. I tried all the systems, the gimmicks, the simple answers, and the few "unsimple" ones I thought I could understand. It was all very demotivating. *Surely,* I remember thinking, *following Jesus ought to have a little fun, a little joy, and a little satisfaction embedded in it. Why do they keep talking about joy when I'm not finding it? What's missing?*

Looking back, I don't ever feel as if anyone fully impressed upon me the fact that the life God blesses is a life lived out of the soul. There it is again: the basic proposition of this book. Wherever it takes us. Life stabilized, nourished, and constantly renewed from this strange uncharted territory deep in the depths of a person. This place called the soul.

I am convinced that there has never been a better time to take a long look at the soul: that place where God meets a person most intimately, speaks in languages that may not have words, and offers the power to perceive reality.

The word *soul* seems to find its way into the language of all sorts of people. Sociologists, philosophers, theologians, artists, and ordinary preachers like me: the list moves steadily ahead from there. Even author Tracy Kidder used the word in a title for a great book, *The Soul of a New Machine*. I take a walk in downtown Boston a few days ago and see a poster advertising a glittery shopping arcade with pricey boutiques. Of the shopping area, the poster blares, "We're the soul of Boston." And a rock station promotes "music for your soul."

These of course are abuses of the term. They take us away from the fact that the soul is something within every one of us—a self—that is unique, God-created, and eternal. It defies science's attempts to locate it (centuries ago scientists tried to weigh the soul by weighing a body before and just after death), to verify it, and to precisely define its function. They couldn't, but that doesn't worry me.

When I speak about the soul in front of people, I find my hands instinctively moving toward my stomach area as if to dramatize the depth of the topic. I don't think of the soul as located in the head. I don't associate it with the pump called a heart in my chest cavity. I'm content to think of it as something beneath all conscious thought, beneath—as someone has said—the trapdoor of the mind.

So there. This soul and how it becomes the place where God blesses the life most dramatically are what I want to write about. This strange part of the "inner space" of a person that exists beyond the body's limitations, beyond physical death. This mystical entity that can be filled with the presence of God, can burst into a mode of praise (as the psalmist said, "Praise the LORD, O my soul"), can feel dreadfully empty, and can become a source of great energy.

As I said, I have known these feelings: the thrill, the emptiness, the energy. And I sense other people talking this language from time to time. I also sense that lots of people are trying to live life without any reference to the soul at all. Soulless lives. Can it be possible?

One can live an entire lifetime, apparently, without ever connecting with the soul. Enough food, enough pleasure, enough stresslessness, enough mental toughness, enough external support, and some can make it through life without ever having to deal with the soul. That doesn't mean they'll get away with it, however. Jesus tells the story of a man who thought that was possible, and on the last day of his life he heard the voice of God saying, "Tonight your soul shall be required of you." Hmmm.

Lots of people have opinions about the soul: what it is, how it differs from the mind and other parts of a person, when it comes to life, and whether or not it lives forever. So that you'll know where I'm coming from, I want you to know what I mean when I use the word *soul* in this book:

- I believe that the soul comes into being at conception. It is not the result of a physical transaction, but it is an event instigated by God in a personal way. God breathes the life of the soul into us.

- I believe that the soul, once created, will never die or lose its identity. It survives the part of us that grows old and capitulates to death.

- I believe that the soul was meant to be the source of life-giving energy, guidance, conviction, connection with the Creator. That it is hardly all of that is the result of sin/evil, which has been passed down like a family curse from the first generation. In short, souls aren't what they used to be.

- I believe that the soul has a certain bottomlessness to it. That it is a place within a person that is similar to boundaryless outer space. Unfortunately, that limitless inner space has been spoiled or polluted by evil. It needs cleansing, redirecting, "rebooting" if it will accomplish anything like the original intention.

- I believe that the soul was meant to be a dwelling place for God. And it can become that again, but there is an effort that is involved.

- I believe that human beings can live as if soulless. That is, they can go a lifetime, if necessary, and never recognize the soul for what it is. To the extent that this happens, they are hollow people.

- As a Christ-follower, I believe that Jesus died to redeem the soul, and that the effect of this redemptive process is to raise life to a higher plane.

Finally, I believe that living out of the soul describes life as God intended it. To live out of the soul is to be in touch with my Creator, to live with an eternal perspective, to live as fully as possible in a mixed-up time.

This book is written to those who want to live out of the soul. To those who want to pursue connection with their innermost parts, who seek to experience the presence of the life of God within.

It's written by one (to borrow words from D. T. Niles) who is a beggar who wants to tell other beggars where they can find bread.

Let me start *The Life God Blesses* with a parable, which is then followed up with a real-time story behind the parable. From there to one or two people I've known who, like myself, have struggled with these questions. And from there to a whole set of ideas about how one makes his or her life open to "blessability."

> Gordon MacDonald
> *Lexington, Massachusetts*
> *Canterbury, New Hampshire*

# A PARABLE

ONCE A FOOLISH man built a boat. His intention was that it would be the grandest, the most talked-about boat that ever sailed from the harbor of the boat club of which he was a member. Thus, he determined to spare no expense or effort.

That the boatbuilder would come to be known as a foolish man had nothing to do with his ability to build, nor did it have to do with his capacity to work hard. It also was not a reference to his personality, for he was a most pleasant person; people often said this. None of this! That he came to be called a foolish man had everything to do with qualities of person—invisible qualities, one might say—that no one was initially able to appreciate. But to say anything more about this is to get ahead of the story.

As he built, the foolish man outfitted his craft with colorful sails, complex rigging, and comfortable appointments and conveniences in its cabin. The decks were made from beautiful teakwood; all the fittings were custom-made of polished brass. And on the stern, painted in gold letters, readable from a considerable distance, was the name of the boat, the *Persona*.

As he built the *Persona*, the foolish man could not resist fantasizing upon the anticipated admiration and applause from club members at the launching of his new boat. In fact, the more he thought about the praise that was soon to come, the more time and attention he gave to those aspects of the boat's appearance that would attract the crowd and intensify excitement.

Now—and this *seems* reasonable—because no one would ever see the underside of the *Persona*, the man saw little need to be concerned about the boat's keel or, for that matter, anything that had to do with the issue of properly distributed weight or ballast. Experienced sailors might wince at this, but one must remember that the boatbuilder was acting with the perceptions of the crowd in his mind—not the seaworthiness of the vessel. Seaworthiness seems not an important issue while in a dry dock.

On one of those occasions when he was sorting out his priorities of time and resources, he said to himself, "Why should I spend money or time on what is out of anyone's sight? When I listen to the conversations of people at the club, I hear them praising only what they can see. I can never remember anyone admiring the underside of a boat. Instead, I sense that my yachting colleagues really find exciting the color and shape of a boat's sails, its brass fittings, its cabin and creature comforts, decks and wood texture, speed and the skill that wins the Sunday afternoon regattas."

So driven by such reasoning, the foolish man built his boat. And everything that would be visible to the people soon began to gleam with excellence. But things that would be invisible when the boat entered the water were generally ignored. People did not seem to take notice of this, or if they did, they made no comment.

The builder's suspicions were correct: the people of the boat club understood and appreciated sails, rigging, decks, brass, and staterooms. And what they saw, they praised. Sometimes he overheard people say that his efforts to build the grandest boat in the history of the club would someday result in his selection as commodore. That had no little effect upon his conviction that he had made good decisions and was on a correct course to boat-club acceptance and success.

When the day came for the boat's maiden voyage, the people of the club joined him at dockside. A bottle of champagne was broken over the bow, and the moment came for the man to set sail. As the breeze filled the sails and pushed the *Persona* from the club's harbor, he stood at the helm and heard what he'd anticipated for years: the cheers and well-wishes of envious admirers who said to one another, "Our club has never seen a grander boat than this. This man will make us the talk of the yachting world." There were some boat owners who joined him, sailing on either side and forming a spectacular flotilla as they moved out beyond the breakwater and into the ocean.

Soon the beautiful *Persona* was merely a blip on the horizon. And as it cut through the swells, its builder and owner, who at this moment seemed anything but a foolish man, gripped the rudder with a feeling of fierce pride. What he had accomplished! He was seized with an increasing rush of confidence that everything—the boat, his future as a boat-club member (and probably as commodore), and even the ocean (why not when one is feeling confident?)—was his to control.

But a few miles out to sea a storm arose. Not a hurricane. But not a squall either. There were sudden wind gusts in excess of forty knots, waves above fifteen feet. The *Persona* began to shudder, and water swept over the sides. Bad things began to happen, and the poise of the "captain" began to waver. Perhaps the ocean wasn't his after all.

How about connections with other club members? The ones who sailed from the harbor on either side, cheering and waving? He looked about for them. But none were to be seen. The boats that had been there in the early part of the voyage had turned back long ago. He'd been too self-absorbed to notice. Besides, other captains knew storm clouds when they saw them.

Within minutes the *Persona's* colorful sails were in shreds, the splendid mast was splintered in pieces, and the rigging was unceremoniously draped all over the bow. The teakwood decks and the lavishly appointed cabin were awash with water. And then before the foolish man could prepare himself, a wave bigger than anything he'd ever seen hurled down upon the *Persona*, and the boat capsized.

Now, this is important! When most boats would have righted themselves after such a battering, the *Persona* did not. Why? Because its builder—this very foolish man—had ignored the importance of what was below the waterline. There was no weight there. In a moment when a well-designed keel and adequate ballast might have saved the ship, they were nowhere to be found. The foolish man had concerned himself with the appearance of things and not enough with resilience and stability in the secret, unseen places where storms are withstood.

Furthermore, because the foolish man had such confidence in his sailing abilities, he had never contemplated the possibility of a situation he could not manage. And that's why later investigations revealed that there were no rescue devices aboard: rafts, life jackets, emergency radios. And the result of this mixture of poor planning and blind pride: the foolish man was lost at sea.

Only when the wreckage of the *Persona* was washed ashore did the drowned man's boat-club friends discover all of this. "Look," they said, "this boat lacks an adequate keel, and there is far more weight above the waterline than below."

They said more! "Only a fool would design and build a boat like this, much less sail in it. A man who builds only above the waterline does not realize that he has built less than half a boat.

Didn't he know that the ocean is dangerous? Didn't he understand that a boat not built with storms in mind is a floating disaster waiting to happen? How absurd that we should have applauded him so enthusiastically."

There were a few old men and women off to one side who heard these things and quietly commented to one another, "We do not remember that anyone mentioned these things when the foolish man was building his *Persona*. What's the use of such questions when his boat is a wreck, and he is nowhere to be found?"

The foolish man was never found. Today, when people speak of him—which is rare—they comment not upon the initial success of the man or upon the beauty of his boat but only upon the silliness of putting out on an ocean where storms are sudden and violent. And doing it with a boat that was really never built for anything else but the vanity of its builder and the praise of spectators. It was in such conversations that the owner of the *Persona*, whose name has long been forgotten, became known as simply the foolish man.

The one who values discernment will ask, "What does this story mean?" and soon discover the answer to the question. And the one who cares little for insight will dismiss the story and likely go out and construct something similar to the foolish man's *Persona*.

And versions of the story go on being recycled in a thousand ways.

> Once a foolish man built a house. . . .
> Once a foolish man built a career. . . .
> Once a foolish man built a marriage. . . .
> Once a foolish man built a life. . . .

# LOST AT SEA

*Major-General Charles George Gordon, C.B.*
*who at all times and everywhere*
*gave his strength to the weak,*
*his substance to the poor,*
*his sympathy to the suffering, his heart to God.*
*—Inscription in St. Paul's Cathedral, London*

IN THE AUTUMN of 1992, Michael Plant, a popular American yachtsman, commenced a solo crossing of the North Atlantic Ocean from the United States to France. But two weeks into the voyage something went amiss, and Plant and his sailboat were lost at sea.

When Plant had prepared to sail, his friends and family had collected at the dock for an enthusiastic farewell. None had reason for anxiety. They were waving good-bye to an expert, one who had circumnavigated the globe alone more than once. The sailing community universally acknowledged Michael Plant as a yachtsman whose seafaring skills were without equal.

Plant's destination had been Les Sables-d'Olonne, France. His midsized sailboat, the *Coyote*, was, as they say, state of the art. The design of its hull, the materials used in its fabrication, the creature comforts: those and every other aspect of his equipment were the epitome of modern sailing lore.

Additionally, Plant had purchased a brand-new 406-megahertz emergency position-indicating radio beacon (Epirb), which was capable of transmitting a message to a satellite in the event of difficulties. Four short signal-bursts from an Epirb radio would be enough for ground stations to determine a fix on the location of the sender and to initiate an immediate rescue.

So one couldn't say that Plant didn't have everything—the best of expertise, experience, and equipment—when he unfurled his sails and put out to sea for Europe. That explains the prevailing assumption of Plant and his friends: nothing could go wrong.

But something did go wrong. Eleven days into the voyage, radio contact with Michael Plant was lost.

Initially, the radio silence raised little alarm. It was known that there were violent storms on the track of Plant's course, and everyone assumed that he was too preoccupied battling the weather to establish contact with his home base. Also, no one—ships at sea, the Coast Guard, airplanes—had reported any SOS or verifiable distress signal, and no news was perceived as good news. It was easy to anticipate that an "everything is OK" message would be forthcoming from the *Coyote* when the seas calmed and Plant was able to settle back into sailing routines.

But when the *Coyote's* radio silence persisted for several days, the confidence of friends and family waned and was replaced by growing apprehension. True, Michael Plant was known as a self-reliant man, but a continuing silence of that duration was out of character even for him. And so there came a moment when decision makers reluctantly concluded that something was amiss.

A search was launched. Airline pilots crossing the ocean were asked to listen for emergency signals; ships in the general area of Plant's course were told to be on the outlook; rescue aircraft from several nations began combing parts of the Atlantic. Days passed with no signals or sightings.

And then the news that no one had ever expected. The *Coyote* was found, floating upside down, by the crew of a freighter 450 miles northwest of the Azores Islands. But no sign of Plant.

Perhaps, some immediately speculated with new hope, the fact that Plant was not with the boat was a sign that he'd survived. Perhaps he was adrift in the emergency inflatable raft that had been stowed in the cabin of his boat.

But even those wishes were frustrated when the *Coyote* was lifted from the water to the deck of the freighter and the raft that might have saved Plant's life was found in the cabin partially inflated and obviously unused. All hopes were destroyed. The fact was that Plant was missing, and there was no clue, nor has there ever been, as to what had happened to him.

Later it was discovered that, eleven days into the voyage, ground stations in Canada and the United States had indeed picked up a distress signal from an Epirb radio. But instead of the four required signal bursts necessary to fix a location, there had been only three. Technicians had been unable to locate the source of the brief transmission and had chosen to ignore it.

Ironies did not stop there. Officials later learned that Plant had installed his new Epirb radio but had not registered its signal with the Coast Guard so that a distress code could have been recognized by computers. One can only guess that the veteran of many similar voyages was so confident of his ability to handle any situation that he treated the matter of personal safety much too casually.

Everyone in the sailing world must have been surprised that, when the *Coyote* was found, it was upside down in the water. Sailboats, it is said, do not capsize . . . normally. They are built to take the most vigorous pounding a sea can offer. Sailors allege that a sailboat is the most natural of all sailing vessels, and it will always right itself even if a wind or wave were to momentarily push it over on its side or even upside down. So why would Michael Plant's sailboat be discovered floating in the Atlantic Ocean upside down? That answer soon became clear.

I'm not a sailor, but I discovered this much about sailboats as I read about Michael Plant's tragedy. I learned that in order for a sailboat to maintain a steady course, and in order for it not to capsize but to harness the tremendous power of the wind, *there must be more weight below the waterline than there is above it.* Any violation of this principle of weight distribution means disaster.

When the *Coyote* was built, an eight-thousand-pound weight was bolted to the keel for this very reason. That kind of ballast below the waterline assured stability. But alter that ratio (permitting more weight above the waterline than below), and the first threatening wind or wave would become a serious problem.

And that is exactly what happened! And here is a further mystery. No one knows why or how, but the eight-thousand-pound weight beneath the waterline broke away from the keel. Did the *Coyote* hit an underwater object? A submarine even? Some ocean debris? Was there a defect in the boatbuilding process? There are no answers, and even as this is written, the issue is being debated in the courts.

The four-ton weight was simply missing, and when that occurred, the boat's stability was compromised. The first wave or wind of any magnitude became the probable deathblow. And when it came, it may have happened so fast that Michael Plant had no time to send any kind of an SOS signal.

No weight below the waterline to ensure stability. No emergency radio in operational condition. No time to take countermeasures. The result? A very capable, experienced, and much admired man lost at sea.

A married couple come to visit with me. They are both graduates of one of America's finest universities. The husband, thanks in part to the support of his wife, has pursued graduate degrees, has launched a successful career, and has attained unusual professional success. His income, they inform me, has flourished every year. Already they have acquired two lovely homes, a weekday condo in the city and a weekend home in the country. A dazzling car with an equally dazzling price tag transports them between the two. It is important to note that their success has not come easily.

They have both worked hard, and the intensity of their efforts is much greater than that of most people I have met. But now there is a crisis in the marriage because the wife has discovered some secret behaviors in her husband's life. His clandestine conduct is totally out of keeping with his professional and intellectual standing. It is not necessary for me to identify the details of what they share with me. One simply needs to say that these are not matters normally connected with someone who has achieved such remarkable success. Needless to say, the behaviors also violate the expectations and covenants of a marital and family lifestyle.

Having been confronted by his wife, the husband has been humiliated and admits that he has no adequate explanation for his actions. All he knows is that suddenly the professional success, the admiration of his colleagues, the accumulation of extraordinary wealth, and the seeming happiness of a marriage and family with children have not been enough to soothe a strange, pulsating restlessness that has lately raged within.

In a short time, everything he has worked for has suddenly become a trap. He no longer enjoys living with it, and he knows that he cannot live without it. So he has unwittingly created a private little world in which he can indulge himself. He is ashamed that he has done this, and he doesn't understand why.

After some visits with the two of them, he and I continue to meet on a weekly basis. I am not a psychologist, but I am fascinated by the story he begins to unfold in response to my questions. He speaks of a childhood in a home marked with verbally abusive parents who consistently reminded him that all bad behavior was evidence that he was useless, lazy, and a disgrace to the family name. He recalls years of school in which almost all of his grades were failures. And he recollects a path of life that was more and more marked by troublesome behavior in the streets.

Then one day in his early teen years, he recounts to me, he climbed a hill that overlooked the town in which he lived and pondered his life and its apparent misdirection. On the hilltop he experienced a blaze of insight and made a personal declaration.

He would rise above all of this mess, he told himself; he would achieve something so stunning and admirable that there would come a day when his parents and their friends would cry to be guests in his splendid home. He would share life with a beautiful wife, servants perhaps, maybe a chauffeured limousine, and membership in the finest clubs.

On the hilltop he fantasized how his parents would apologize for their abusiveness, and how they would tell him that he had made them proud. The neighbors also: people who had known this troublesome kid would speak of how they remembered him and how far he had come. They would line up to ask favors of him.

It was a remarkable dream, his hilltop vision. Some would call it a kind of conversion experience. And it offered more than enough motivational energy to get him started and to keep him going for the next twenty years through graduate school and through the difficult years of launching his career. Within a short time of that hilltop experience, grades rose from failures to "excellents." Laziness turned to industriousness, and behavior altered from intransigent to impeccable.

And the hilltop vision came true. Soon there were indeed graduate school and scholarships. Then recognition. The admiring, so very capable wife. A young adult career path marked with opportunities and connections and a subsequent level of success that exceeded even the wildest fantasies in the hilltop experience back home. Indeed, the parents and neighbors did come to praise his achievements. And just as he'd once anticipated, they spoke— usually in jest—of his earlier days and how far he'd come. And they asked for favors.

So why then this strange restlessness of heart that became the base for unexplained temptations and conduct at an age when one should know better? How can I get him to step back from life in real time and think through where this track of living has brought him? Could the sailor's parable fit here? Would it provide him with the kind of vocabulary of thought necessary to reevaluate where he is headed? I think so.

And that's why one day as we talk together I tell him the story of Michael Plant and his loss of life out on the Atlantic Ocean. At first he is mystified as to why I would have interrupted our intense conversation about his personal struggles with a tale of the sea. But then I get to the matter of the weight below the waterline. I ask him if there is any parallel between his present situation and that of Plant's boat when it lost its weight below the waterline.

He nods reflectively as he begins to perceive that he may have spent his years building up the rigging, the sails, and the mast of life. The good life: it's all there to be admired and enjoyed. But there's almost nothing below the waterline! Something deep within is empty, alone. For the first time in our conversations we have reached a point where we can begin to talk about a most mysterious dimension of life: the soul—the inner "place" that defies the best efforts of philosophers and theologians who seek a satisfying definition.

The soul, I suggest to him, is somewhere below the personal waterline. And it is easily ignored until the Atlantic (or Galilean) storms of life arise. And if there is no weight at the level of the soul, there is little to promise survival.

We go back across the years and speak again of the energy

that developed out of a painful childhood and how it was diverted into the building of a career, wealth, and notoriety. And we conclude that all this frantic building—like that of a foolish man—was done above the waterline. Admirable! To be envied! But good only as long as there were no storms.

But now the storms had arisen. And in a strange way.

"I have a thought for you," I had said to my visitor one day. "I want you to remember the good-for-nothing kid who climbed the hill that day. Did you actually think that you left that scruffy kid behind when you went back down the hill with new intentions? That kid who was kicked around, who felt out of whack with everything, who was angry and hurt, who wanted to prove his worth? Did you really think you could just walk away from him?"

His answer was a positive nod of the head. Yes, he finally answered, he had thought that the unattractive, failure-driven kid could be left at the top of the hill. And hadn't he been left there after all? Hadn't someone new walked back down that hillside? Don't the career and its professional standing, the homes, the cars, and the beautiful family prove that?

"Then why are we here, twenty-five years later, talking about some very secretive and stupid behaviors?" I ask.

"I guess because in running away from the kid I once was, I've only been building above the waterline all these years."

# STORMS HAPPEN

*Those people who influence us most
are not those who buttonhole us and
talk to us, but those who lived their
lives like the stars of heaven and the
lilies in the field, perfect, simply, and
unaffectedly. Those are the lives that
mold us.*
*—Oswald Chambers*

NOT BEING A man of the sea, I learned from the Michael Plant story all I have ever known about the significance of keels and proper weight distributions below the waterline of sailboats. It also underscored what I'd heard from other sources. The sea is never taken for granted by the experienced sailor, even in the best sailing craft. Out on the sea one always assumes that storms will happen. And the worst along with them.

And storms happen in real life. In spite of the fact that new generations are entering our world who don't appear to know that or really want to face its truth. These are generations—in the Western society, of course—who learned somewhere that life is to be lived without pain, without struggle, without inconvenience.

"You have to understand that my generation entered adulthood with the assumption that we would all have good jobs that paid more each year, career tracks that had no limits, marriages that would never grow dull or troublesome, and bodies that would never fail us. I'm forty-two now. I've got friends who've been laid off of work, friends whose marriages are just plain awful, and friends who are having ulcers and heart attacks. A lot of us just don't know how to face all of this. We're just downright depressed."

These are words spoken to me across a breakfast table at Friendly's in Lexington, Massachusetts, one of the places I meet men for breakfast almost every morning of the week. They are spoken by a forty-two-year-old man I like very, very much. A man who is smart and who has grown up as a confessing Christ-follower. He is being quite vulnerable as he speaks of accumulated disillusionments in his own private world.

I tell him about Michael Plant, too, and go on to borrow and modify a somewhat offensive phrase frequently seen on bumper stickers and sweatshirts, "Storms happen." They've happened to me, I say, and you can anticipate them coming in increasing quantities as the years pass.

"You're not being very encouraging about the prospect of getting older," he says with a rueful grin.

"I was thinking the other day about our Christmas letters," I respond. "When Gail and I were in our late twenties, our thirties, and our early forties, the letters would pour in at every Christmastime with amazing amounts of good news from all our friends. As they recapped the year, they would say, 'I got married to the most wonderful man this year . . . ,' or 'Mary Ann and I moved to San Diego this past year and bought a lovely home. We're so fortunate that . . . ,' or 'Our little Todd got the highest batting average on his Little League team and . . . ,' or 'Tom [or Sharon] got a tremendous promotion this year, and it looks like. . . .' You ever get those kinds of letters?"

"Yeah, we've gotten them."

I go on, "But what's impressed Gail and me is how they're changing."

"What do you mean?"

"Well, we're in our fifties now. And the Christmas letters

include a lot of mixed news: 'I'm sorry to have to tell you that Mary Ann and I separated this past year and . . . ,' or 'Todd dropped out of college this year, he was married in November, and he and his new wife have a baby girl . . . ,' or 'These have been difficult months for us since Sharon [or Tom] got laid off. Economic conditions here are. . . .' What I'm saying is that the same people who had only good news earlier on now have lots of bad news to share. Sooner or later almost everyone gets tested by storms."

My friend at Friendly's does not greet my observation with glee.

When storms happen, we learn more about what's below the waterline of our own existence than we could have learned in any other way. One exception, perhaps. We may learn just as much, if not more, when this boat that symbolizes our being is put into dry dock and fully exposed above and below the waterline. But more of this idea just a bit later.

"Sub-waterline issues" seem so unimportant when the seas are calm and the winds are favorable. So *it's only when the storms hit and something catastrophic happens* that we are likely to ask a different set of questions. Why wasn't the weight better distributed? we ask. What happened to that keel? Where did the boat's designer or the boat's builders make their mistakes? And once the boat was launched, why wasn't the radio operational and properly registered? Why would an experienced man sail into a potentially stressful situation for which he was not optimally prepared?

In the early months of President Bill Clinton's administration, a close friend who had been appointed to his staff, Vincent Foster, Jr., left his White House office early one afternoon and ended his life at a parkway rest stop along the Potomac River. The Clintons and officials in Washington were left in shock. Why would a man at the peak of his career, called to Washington to serve alongside a lifelong friend, kill himself without apparent warning?

In the weeks that followed, a mass of "sub-waterline questions" cascaded through the press. What had been going on inside this man that caused him so much despair that he terminated his life? Why hadn't people closest to him seen the signs that he was in terrible internal agitation? Was it because in hard-driving, achievement-oriented Washington, people are usually too busy to look beneath the waterline and pursue a reality check?

I avidly read all the press reports that I could find on Vincent Foster, Jr. I kept looking for mention of any one person who might have been close enough to him to have noted a look of pain in his eyes or who might have had enough discernment to pick up in his tone of voice a cry of pain. But if there was anyone of that sort, he or she was never mentioned.

Edward Arlington Robinson's poem, it seems to me, describes the Vincent Foster, Jr., situation all too well:

> Whenever Richard Cory went down town,
> We people on the pavement looked at him:
> He was a gentleman from sole to crown,
> Clean favored, and imperially slim.
>
> And he was always quietly arrayed,
> And he was always human when he talked;
> But still he fluttered pulses when he said,
> "Good morning," and he glittered when he walked.
>
> And he was rich—yes, richer than a king—
> And admirably schooled in every grace.
> In fine, we thought that he was everything
> To make us wish that we were in his place.
>
> So on we worked, and waited for the light,
> And went without the meat, and cursed the bread;
> And Richard Cory, one calm summer night,
> Went home and put a bullet through his head.

Throughout the millennia, there has been a genre of reflective people who didn't wait for a storm of the Michael Plant (a meteorological storm) variety or the Vincent Foster (a psychic storm) variety to tell us how important it was to give attention to affairs below life's waterline.

Sometimes these people have been called the spiritual masters or masters of the inner life, meaning that they have believed in looking inward—exploring the depth of their own person—in their attempts to measure reality. They have properly discerned that the sub-waterline space of life remains to this day the most unexplored space in the universe.

It is said that many ancient mapmakers indicated unexplored territory with drawings of threatening dragons and the words *ne plus ultra,* meaning "nothing beyond." And I am tempted to think with dismay that here we are at the threshold of the twenty-first century, and the deep inwardness of man remains similarly an unconquered frontier to a considerable extent.

This inner space that has captivated the interest of the spiritual masters is often called the soul or the heart, and it describes the part of every human being that cannot be physically located or measured. I would venture the almost mystical notion that the soul—this inner space—is as infinite in size as we perceive outer space to be. If we measure outer space in terms of light-years, we may measure the size of the soul in terms of eternity, a timeless measurement that understandably baffles the mind.

Some do prefer the word *heart* or *spirit* to the word *soul.* The biblical writers and Jesus Himself were comfortable with all three. No matter: we are using mere words to describe something that bends to no definition and, as I said, sends the mind into unsettling mysteries.

The spiritual masters have always been a unique lot. They have worried little about appearances above life's waterline because they found so much to discover beneath it. Therefore, they have usually been regarded as strange, impractical, out of touch, and threatening.

Only infrequently have these sorts of people enjoyed any sort of renown, and that usually because—you guessed it—a storm of sorts arose among their contemporaries. A storm that challenged the minds and resources of those in the habit of being in control. In such moments panicky and anguished people have turned to the masters with questions: What does this mean? What should we do? Do you think that heaven speaks here?

The Older Testament prophet Isaiah should certainly be counted among the spiritual masters. He lived in a time replete with storms of political, economic, and religious kinds. In his time one head of state, Ahaz, became numbed with fear because of invading armies that threatened to engulf his kingdom: the heart of Ahaz was "moved as the trees of the woods are moved with the wind" (Isa. 7:2). Note the below-the-waterline reference to Ahaz's condition.

But not so with Isaiah:

> The LORD spoke thus to me with a strong hand, and instructed
> me that I should not walk in the way of this people, saying:
> "Do not say, 'A conspiracy,'
> Concerning all that this people call a conspiracy,
> Nor be afraid of their threats,
>   nor be troubled.
> The LORD of hosts, Him you shall hallow;
> Let Him be your fear,
> And let Him be your dread" (Isa. 8:11–13).

Isaiah's comments illustrate soul-talk. Ahaz is a man who has lived his life soullessly and suddenly realizes that he is in a life-threatening situation. He's in a violent storm, one could say, and he needs the help of someone who is conversant with deeper things, territory where the Creator speaks. And that's why a spiritual master is usually the person you want to have around when the storms whip up. It's in the storm that you find out where are the lives God has blessed.

Spiritual masters come in all sorts, sizes, and shapes. In history one could often find them in quiet places such as deserts and forests where they would not be distracted by the sights and sounds of commercial man and his activities. If there were men and women who insisted on exploring uncharted seas, unknown continents, and untouched moons and planets, the spiritual masters were drawn to the inner regions of the person and proposing that there is an infinity of sorts within every human being.

The spiritual masters, then and now, believe that this below-the-waterline part of human life is tragically neglected. Here it is, they like to say, that one finds the most satisfying relationship with God. This is the place where a healthy integration of all the personal systems of life might take place. When fully functional, it is the place where convictions and values are birthed, where courage, hope, perseverance, and stability are generated.

Some of the masters referred to this sub-waterline part of the person as the still point; others, the deep center or an inner garden or a shrine for worship. And some whose exploration of the soul has been disciplined in the biblical tradition—as is mine—like to take note of God's insistence that the people of Israel, who had so much to learn about their saving God, construct a tabernacle that would always be located in the center of their community. And the center of the elaborately designed tent was a place called the Holy of Holies. God's presence and His glory were said to be there.

More than a few have speculated that the sacred place was meant to be an object lesson to point people toward even more sacred space within them.

No one understood the inner depths of a person better than Jesus of Nazareth, Jesus the Christ. He came in a time and among a people who seem to have become content with a lifestyle that put form and appearance over substance. What enraged His critics from the very beginning was His insistence that all conversations be centered on matters of the soul.

"He knew what was in man," John says of Jesus. And that must have been maddening to men who had spent their lives decorating their outer lives with the ornaments of religiosity, power, and wealth. I mean, how do you respond to a person who cares nothing about how much you know concerning the Law and the Prophets, how well connected you are to the temple infrastructure, how many prayers you pray in a day's time, and how many pilgrimages you've made? What defense do you put up when someone looks into the center of your soul and causes you to face up to the evil and sleaze that reside within?

If there is a deeper reason for crucifying Jesus than just that He was a threat to the religious structure and that He enjoyed the affections of the common class, it is that He forced men to look into their souls and face the inadequacies there.

Conversely, it is why others loved and followed Him. Because they came to realize that He was less interested in their reputations as prostitutes and tax collectors and more drawn to the sorrow that lay in their souls and their desire to be liberated from the deadening evil that proscribed their lives up until that point. They wanted clean souls, and Jesus was in a position to help them through forgiveness and redemption. That was His gospel.

*But what if this inner part of the human being is ignored?* If not ignored, then polluted? If not polluted, then blasphemed? What if (and here my metaphor of things above and below the waterline fails to assist) it is possible for one to lose touch with his or her soul? Or to put it another way, what if the modern person with all of his or her emphasis upon rationalism, hedonism, and materialism has taken leave of the soul and the faintest connection (like a bad phone line) barely exists?

The result, I suggest, is a strangely hollow person, almost an automated kind of human being who spends most of life simply responding to events and circumstances, to glands, instincts, and passions or ambitions beyond explanation.

Frederick Buechner writes sadly of his mother who died a very lonely death as an old woman. She seems to fit the description of one who never looked below the waterline. Of her he writes,

> [She] was by no means heartless, but I think hers was a heart that, who knows why, was rarely if ever touched in its deepest place. To let it be touched there was a risk that for reasons known only to her she was apparently not prepared to take.

Because there was a sense of hollowness within, her last years—when storms can often be at their worst—were marked with sadness:

> Being beautiful was her business, her art, her delight, and it took her a long way and earned her many dividends, but when, as she saw it, she lost her beauty . . . she was like a millionaire who runs out of money. She took her name out of the phone book and got an unlisted number. . . . With her looks gone she felt she had nothing left to offer the world, to propitiate the world. So what she did was simply to check out of the world   that old, last rose of summer   the way Greta Garbo and Marlene Dietrich checked out of it, holing themselves up somewhere and never venturing forth except in disguise. My mother holed herself up in her apartment . . . then in just one room of that apartment, then in just one chair in that room, and finally, in the bed where one morning a few summers ago, perhaps in her sleep, she died at last.

In our generation an overwhelming majority seem to be trying to live above the waterline with scant reference to the soul. They have been *converted* (and that is indeed the word) to the opinion that one's skill, one's IQ, one's connection to family, friends, and a good university, and one's chutzpah or nerve are all that count to make sense out of reality. And all too often, this actually appears to work quite well unless there is a storm. So it is not unusual for people to march through life and give little, if any, consideration to matters below the waterline—to live in the region of the soul.

Jesus was getting at this when He told a crowd: "One's life does not consist in the abundance of the things he possesses" (Luke 12:15). He backed up His point with a simple story. A rich man has enjoyed a prosperous harvest and is overwhelmed with profits. His remarkable prosperity offers a problem. What should he do about all of this that is so abundant above the waterline of his life?

His solution? A typical above-waterline one. Build more barns, store the stuff, and retire to good living. "Take your ease," Jesus quotes him as saying, "Eat, drink, and be merry."

> But God said to him, "Fool! This night your soul will be required of you; then whose will those things be which you have provided?" (Luke 12:19–20).

Jesus isn't specific about how this encounter happened. After all it's just a story. But then again it may have been a true story. Maybe most people in the crowd knew the very man of whom Jesus spoke. They knew about the harvests, the barns, the man's retirement plans. And well they could because these are the things we see and hear about successful people. The part they could not have seen or heard, however, was the conversation the man had with

God. Because that would have happened privately, below the waterline, in the space of the soul.

How had the man died? Heart attack perhaps. Stroke, murder, or a chariot accident. Whatever! It was simply a moment in which a storm happened. The cause of the death is not important to Jesus; but the meaning of the death is.

I would like to refer to this "stormy" experience in the rich man's life (or end of his life) as a "disruptive moment." Like Michael Plant's Atlantic storm, like Vincent Foster, Jr.'s sudden terrible disillusionment with Washington life, like Richard Cory's encounter with suffocating loneliness, and like Ahaz's paralyzing fear over the threat to his kingdom, a disruptive moment occurs when someone is pressed or forced to look below the waterline for explanations, for stabilizing assistance, for significance, and for truth and wisdom.

The rich man in Jesus' story could be most of us. Few exceptions. If we live in a context of abundance, we are most likely to be found in his track of thought. Our preoccupation gravitates toward things above the waterline, not below. And we are drawn to matters concerning what is below only when something of the nature of an Atlantic storm arises.

Anyone familiar with the life of Jesus remembers when He and His disciples were crossing Lake Galilee and were overtaken by a storm of life-threatening proportions. There is something profoundly instructive in the fact that the Lord was asleep at the stern of the boat while the disciples—some of them experienced fishermen—were beside themselves with fear in the bow. And when they concluded that things were out of control, they crawled (my imagination chooses this word) to where Jesus was and pressed Him with one question: Don't You care if we drown?

For some unknown reason it never dawned upon me until ecently that the disciples' question was probably more practical than miracle oriented. Now, I hear them saying, "We're all [You and us] about to drown. How can You sleep through this when we need all the help we can get? Wake up and help us row or bail water or something."

It must have been a bit unnerving to them to feel so threatened only to look back and find Jesus oblivious to everything that was transpiring. Thus, their question.

The writers of the story speak of Jesus awakening, speaking to the storm, and causing it to submit to His word. Instantly: stillness, calm, clear sky(?). And then this question addressed to the men in the boat: Where is your faith?

In other words, we know what's above the waterline in your lives—fear. But what's below? Answer: apparently very little in the way of resource. That's the redeeming virtue of storms: they force open the doors of the soul, show what's there.

Recently, Gail and I spent a month in South Africa. There we met some of the most remarkable men and women, strong, lovers of God, courageous, and committed to the building of a new South Africa. One of our hosts, George Irvine, then the Methodist bishop of the Grahamstown District, told us of a black pastor in his district whose home was firebombed and destroyed one night.

Early in the morning the bishop went out to the township and found the pastor and his family standing at the front of their burned-out home. Nothing was left but the chimney. All personal belongings, furniture, books, and sermon notes were gone. Only the clothes they were wearing were left.

The bishop said as he looked on the ruins of their home, he suddenly noticed that the pastor had done one thing that might reveal the determination of his heart. For there on the chimney wall, the only part left standing, the pastor had taken a lump of charcoal and written the words that were spoken as a vow by all Methodist pastors each year at the District Conference:

Put me to what you will,
Put me to doing,
Put me to suffering,
Let me be laid aside for you,
Let me have all things,
Let me have nothing.
I freely and heartily yield
All things to your pleasure and disposal.

# STORMS
# AND DISRUPTIVE MOMENTS

*A new Everest Expedition—the
weekly Times of September 8. I have
been reading Sir Francis
Younghusband. He asks and answers
the stock question, Who will be one
ounce the better for it? This is part of
his answer. . . .*

*Everest has become a symbol. Everest
stands for all that is highest, purest,
and most difficult of attainment. As
the climbers struggle gasping towards
the summit they will be putting heart
into all who are striving upward in
whatever field. This knowledge will do
most to put heart into themselves. So,
in the words of Somervell, written on
the day after his splendid failure:
"The fight is worth it—worth it
every time."*
*—Amy Carmichael*

I AM OLD enough to appreciate how the interstate freeway system
has changed American automobile travel. A multiple of lanes,
graceful curves, large informative green signs, and frequent rest
stops (which seem to all look alike) are parts of a distinctive modern

transportation network built in just the last few decades. The interstates are designed to make it possible for anyone to drive nonstop from one end of the continent to the other with minimal stress. On the other hand, there is a high boredom factor on such a drive.

Advice: keep awake, within the speed limit, gassed up, and you'll get where you want to go pain-free and bleary-eyed. Oh, and you'll also have learned next to nothing on your journey.

For me the greater fascination is with secondary roads, most of which, before the interstates, were the actual primary routes. The secondaries wind through small towns and villages that the interstates avoid, and they usually follow the contours of the countryside. You see things on secondary roads, and so even though it takes more time and caution, I like to drive them whenever possible.

Now, unlike the interstates, secondary roads do not promise unhindered passage. Sometimes they're poorly maintained, and the ride can be bumpy. Each town seems to have one police officer with a radar unit designed to raise revenues from hapless passersby. And you better be prepared for the inevitable slow-moving vehicle that can keep you crawling for miles along no-passing zones. On the secondaries your ability to predict the exact hour in which you will reach your destination is limited. There are too many potential disruptions along the way.

My personal life has the appearance of travel on one of these secondary roads. A map of the routes I've lived on would show almost no straight lines or freeways anywhere. A log of my life's travels would note experiences reminiscent of detours, accidents, flat tires, potholes, and speeding tickets. But it would also show that there have been glorious vistas, roadside parks, delightful towns and villages all symbolizing the marvelous discoveries, great friendships, and opportunities to make a difference that I've enjoyed. Although I have admired and applauded those who seem to have lived an interstate lifestyle, I have not, and I'm not sad about it.

This personal map of mine with its secondary roads and their crazy surprises around each curve is dotted with what I call disruptive moments: those unanticipated events, most of which, one would usually have chosen to avoid had it been possible.

When I have reflected upon the disruptive moments marked on my personal road map of life, I have noted that most of them became occasions for what I'd like to call soul-talk, the sort of conversation Jesus often had with His disciples on the heels of a disappointment or a failure. Jesus, the master Teacher, was always quick to follow every event with questions that were meant to search the soul for its motives and its intentions.

Soul-talk: those unforgettable, sometimes life-changing (at the least life-stabilizing) conversations between God and myself, myself and others. And looking back, I have also come to realize that in those disruptive moments—as some like to say—a wake-up call alerted me that some aspect of my sub-waterline life was in a state of neglect. That's why, as I enter the last third of my life, I gain an increasingly appreciative perspective about these disruptive moments.

This is not a rule, please understand, only an observation. But I cannot avoid noting that most of us—human beings that we are—are inclined to neglect the soul and all else beneath the waterline *unless* or *until* these disruptive moments come. We don't like disruptive moments; they are too often associated with pain and inconvenience, failure and humiliation. Not that they have to be, but that seems the way of the human condition.

Malcolm Muggeridge seemed to be thinking about this when in a conversation with William Buckley he said,

As an old man, Bill, looking back on one's life, it's one of the things that strikes you most forcibly—that the only thing that's taught one anything is suffering. Not success, not happiness, not anything like that. The only thing that really teaches one what life's about—the joy of understanding, the joy of coming in contact with what life really signifies—is suffering, affliction.

Throughout the pages of autobiography, one finds descriptions of disruptive moments that led people into new thoughts and insights. In his autobiography Bertrand Russell writes of a moment like this when his wife was dying:

She seemed cut off from everyone and everything by walls of agony, and the sense of the solitude of each human soul suddenly overwhelmed me. Ever since my marriage my emotional life had been calm and superficial. I had forgotten all the deeper issues, and had been content with flippant cleverness. Suddenly the ground seemed to give way beneath me, and I found myself in quite another region. Within five minutes I went through some reflections as the following: the loneliness of the human soul is unendurable; nothing can penetrate it except the highest intensity of the sort of love that religious teachers have preached; whatever does not spring from this motive is harmful, or at best useless; it follows that war is wrong; that a public school education is abominable, that the use of force is to be deprecated, and that in human relations one should penetrate to the core of loneliness in each person and speak to that.

I include Russell's comments because I want to point out that disruptive moments are not exclusive to people who have organized their lives about the Bible and Jesus Christ. People are apt to have these profound moments of insight for any reason, at any time. Where a disruptive moment leads is anyone's guess. But it is nevertheless a time, perhaps unlike any other, when one is more apt to move into communion with God and be receptive to the most searing truths about self and the world. When this happens, it has usually occurred at what I call soul-level.

I can't help thinking that the most startling (and amusing) disruptive moment in all of biblical literature comes in the complicated story of Balaam riding on his donkey. There is a moment when it is apparent that God wishes to lead him into deeper discernments of the situation facing him, and he is not listening. But his donkey is! Which is instructive.

Several times the donkey resists Balaam's directives, turning off the road and even running him into a wall so that his foot is crushed. And on three occasions Balaam beats the donkey into submission. Balaam doesn't seem to know (and certainly doesn't see) that an angelic messenger stands in the path. The humorous side of the story rises because the donkey is aware of the angel and wants to do what its master ought to do: namely, to stop and listen.

Finally, the donkey simply lies down, and Balaam loses control and starts beating his faithful beast with his staff. This prompts the donkey to speak ("Then the LORD opened the mouth of the donkey"), and it says to Balaam, "What have I done to you, that you have struck me these three times?"

There is no indication that Balaam is amazed by this event because he immediately answers back, "Because you have abused me. I wish there were a sword in my hand, for now I would kill you!" The conversation between Balaam and his donkey moves on until God opens Balaam's eyes, and he sees what his donkey had already seen: the angel. "And he bowed his head and fell flat on his face." Which is standard operating procedure in a disruptive moment. When he is faced with the implications of his resistance, he can only comment, "I have sinned." (See Num. 22:21–35.)

The story is not so funny if one looks beneath its surface and realizes that Balaam's performance is parallel to that of those who ride through life as if on an interstate freeway, quite unaware of or unanticipating God's attempts to reach out and connect. That is why the majority of disruptive moments seem to be framed in pain and difficult circumstance because—as in Balaam's case—God seems to allow trauma in order to make us open to a little talk at soul-level.

More than a few have noted the power in the words of Solzhenitsyn who, in referring to a disruptive moment(s) in his own life in the Gulag, wrote,

> It was only when I lay there on rotting prison straw that I sensed within myself the first stirrings of good. Gradually, it was disclosed to me that the line separating good and evil passes, not through states, nor between classes, nor between political parties either, but right through every human heart, and through all human hearts. So bless you, prison, for having been in my life.

So like the great Russian writer, I have gradually become thankful for my disruptive moments. They have forced me inward and downward into soul territory. My journals suggest that almost every useful encounter I have had with God has occurred in the wake of a disruptive moment. And as a result, I have not since been the same.

In one of the worst moments of my life—the most profound of all the "disruptions"—a friend took me to breakfast. As I remember his words, they went like this: "You might not understand now, and I may even make you angry by saying this, but I believe that you will look back someday and give thanks for a time like this." Looking back to the moment, I said this: "I remember a small part of me (not made of God) wanting to punch him." But in the perspective of time I know him to be right: I didn't understand, and he is right: I do give thanks for those days . . . now.

So the possibility of disruptive moments—those times we all like to avoid—drives a question or two:

- What kinds of disruptive moments are there?
- Are any of them good, or are they all painful?
- And what does one do to harvest a disruptive moment for all of its potential value?

In another book, *Rebuilding Your Broken World*, I recalled the same disruptive moment mentioned in the last paragraphs: again, a time filled with personal anguish and humiliation. Another trusted friend sat with my wife, Gail, and me and said this: "The two of you are walking through a terribly painful period in your life. You have a choice. Either you will make every attempt to deny or avoid the pain or you will accept the necessity of walking straight through it until the end. Yes, it will hurt, but through it all, God will say things to you that you may never have heard otherwise. The first choice leaves you with nothing but emptiness; the second choice offers growth and depth you could not have imagined."

We consciously chose the second of the two. And enough years have now passed for us to understand that our friend's counsel was correct.

When I am in conversation with a person whom I am just getting to know, and if I feel that we have reached a point of reasonable trust, I like to ask this question: "Have you ever gone through an experience in which you felt you were totally broken?"

Usually, the answer is yes. Just a few days before writing these paragraphs, I asked the question to a young man, and his answer was an immediate yes.

"All my life I anticipated playing football in the NFL," he said. "When I reached the end of my college career, I was drafted by the ———[and he mentioned a team]. I went off to training and was soon convinced that I was as good as anyone on the field. I expected to gain a starting position real quick once the season began. Then one day without warning I was called to the coach's office."

Here my friend mentioned one of the best-known football coaches in the world. "I sat down in his office. Neither of us could look at the other in the eye. The coach said, 'We're going to have to let you go.' That was it: 'We're going to have to let you go.' In a few minutes I found myself out in the parking lot headed for my car. And suddenly it hit me: I'd been cut. My football days were over. And I sat on the ground by my car and cried. But in the next hour God was able to speak to me about my life for the first time."

I heard David Burnham, a well-traveled spiritual coach to athletes, tell a similar story. "The football was my god," he said. "And one day in a championship game, I was carrying the ball into the line and was hit so hard that I was knocked unconscious. They had to carry me off the field and to an ambulance. I came to while they were loading me into the ambulance behind the stadium. And the first thing I heard was the crowd roaring for another ball carrier. My god was in another man's arms, and the crowd was on to other heroes."

These are samples—dramatic ones—of disruptive moments. The time when the soul is suddenly capable of hearing.

My personal experiences and my observations of others who have permitted me access to their inner lives suggest to me that there are probably four kinds of disruptive moments leading to sensitivity about things below the waterline.

## The Disruptive Moment of Crisis:
### *The Thing We Cannot Control*

It is an overused word, *crisis*. It refers to any event, usually negative, for which we are unprepared. But I cannot find a better one. *Crisis describes an event that we cannot control.* Most often disruptive moments that are crisis-driven are traumatic and overwhelming.

One is reminded of the floods that have frequently dominated the lives of American midwesterners. Tens of millions of dollars have been spent to build dams and levees to hold back the waters of the great midwestern rivers. Engineers have celebrated their accomplishments by calling these dams one-hundred-year dams, meaning that they are meant to hold back the worst conceivable floods that might happen in one hundred years.

But what if—as in one recent case—the flood is not a one-hundred-year flood but a five-hundred-year flood? That once-in-half-a-millennium event that no one thought was possible in his or her lifetime? That is truly a disruptive event. And it leaves everyone scrambling, heartbroken, desperate.

Sooner or later most of us face a crisis of this sort. We come up against something we cannot control. And this is what happened to Michael Plant. We can surmise that he thought he and his boat, the *Coyote*, could handle anything the Atlantic could throw at them. And perhaps his was a reasonable assumption and would have remained so *if* his keel with its attached eight-thousand-pound weight had been dependable.

Most of us can trace back across the years of our lives and describe a mountain range of crises—some greater or taller than others. I have known the crises of watching my parents dissolve a twenty-five-year marriage, of almost flunking out of college because in my youthfulness I lacked the will to persevere in difficult times, of helplessly watching our two-year-old daughter come close to death (or potential brain damage) because she had mistaken whitened turpentine for milk in a cereal bowl. I remember the crises of severe financial stress, of a severe moment of personal despair that made me wonder if I was losing my mind, of a disappointment so bewildering that I found myself questioning if I knew how to hear God's voice at all.

But no crisis in my life has equaled a time several years ago when I engaged in a sequence of choices that eventuated in a total personal failure. It was a disruptive moment that featured betrayal, shame and humiliation, the apparent loss of all things (except my family and some incredibly faithful friends). And the result was the pain I mentioned just a page or two ago.

It was crisis—the five-hundred-year storm—the disruptive moment in all of its fury. And one faces what the poet Robert Frost once called those "two roads diverged in a yellow wood." The road to the left is quite often marked with denial, defensiveness, blaming, and escape. And the road to the right is marked with repentance, sorrow, submission, and quiet.

The renowned Presbyterian preacher Clarence McCartney, of Pittsburgh, once said, "The anguish of a Christian soul who has been betrayed by Satan into sin is far keener and greater than that of one who sins continuously and without distress or compunction of conscience." In my disruptive moment of crisis, I came to understand McCartney's words.

Crisis suggests a period of life when we discover that all of our battery of strengths so carefully massed in better times are inadequate for this powerful storm. The crisis may be of our own making (as was mine), or it may be the convergence of unpredictable events we could not have seen coming before it was too late: a cancer diagnosis, a betrayal by a friend, an economic downturn that stifles a career, a severe accident, the death of someone we dearly love.

In a book called *Who Speaks for God?*, Charles Colson comments on a question asked him by an Australian interviewer: "Mr. Colson, you are an unusual person. You have conquered the pinnacles of secular success. The goals most people strive their whole lives for, you have achieved—only to see it all collapse as you fell from the White House to prison. But now you're out, leading a new life as a Christian. It's like having lived two lives. How would you sum up the meaning of those two lives?"

Colson wrote that he had only twenty seconds to answer. "If my life stands for anything," he said quickly, "it is the truth of the teaching of Jesus Christ, '. . . whoever wants to save his life will lose it, but whoever loses his life for Me will find it. What good will it be for a man if he gains the whole world, yet forfeits his soul?'"

Colson went on to comment on his answer: "I had spent my first 40 years seeking the whole world, to the neglect of my soul. But what I couldn't find in my quest for power and success—that is, true security and meaning—I discovered in prison, where all worldly props had been stripped away. And by God's grace, I lost my life in order that I might find true life in Christ."

This is crisis—the disruptive moment—and in Colson's case, it was the beginning of his finest hours. It forced him below the waterline to discover that inner space and what possibilities there might be there for him if he connected with God.

### The Disruptive Moment of Wonderment:
*The Thing We Cannot Explain*

If crisis describes a moment we cannot control, *wonderment (or astonishment) describes a moment we cannot explain.* A moment that is disruptive because it leaves us breathless, stupefied.

Moments of wonderment cause us to realize again that there are systems of reality beyond our understanding. We ponder them, and our thinking system slides into rebellion. To use computer language, the mind sends up an "error message" as if to say, "This can't be, for I did not and cannot think of it first." Or the mind says, "This is too wonderful, and its cause or its message exceeds my capacity to appreciate."

In his autobiography Whittaker Chambers describes a personal disruptive moment when he was holding his newborn daughter in his arms:

> My eye came to rest on the delicate convolutions of her ear—those intricate, perfect ears. The thought passed through my mind: "no, those ears were not created by any chance coming together of atoms in nature (the communist view). They could have been created only by immense design." The thought was involuntary and unwanted. I crowded it out of my mind. But I never wholly forgot it or the occasion. I did not then know that, at that moment, the finger of God was first laid upon my forehead.

Perhaps the Chambers experience touches me so much because I had a similar one when my daughter-in-law, Patty, called one day and invited Gail and me to join her at the doctor's office. Patty was six months pregnant with our first granddaughter, Erin Gail, and she wanted us to be with her when the doctor checked on the baby's health with the use of a sonogram.

At first I resisted the invitation, saying that such things were for women only, but Patty was persuasive and on the appointed day I was there with Gail to meet her. We were brought into a semi-darkened room. Off to one side was a machine with a screen much like a television. Suddenly, the screen came to life, and we began seeing the outline of a baby: arms, legs, head. The doctor began to zoom in on parts of the body of a child we would later come to know as Erin Gail. We saw fingers and fingernails. We saw eyes, nose, and mouth. The doctor pointed out the heart, and we saw it beating. There were the spinal column and other aspects of bone structure. Everything, the doctor noted, was normal.

But nothing was normal for me. I stood speechless. I could not take my eyes off that screen and the child that was in our daughter-in-law's womb. I watched as Erin Gail slowly moved her legs and arms in response to the machine's stimulation. She was a whole, healthy, and very much alive human being. Within months I would hold her in my arms and offer a blessing. And I was awed and wept.

It was a disruptive moment, there in the doctor's office. I can think of very few other moments like it in all of my life. We were peering into a mother's body and seeing life grow. We were seeing the way God prepares His sons and daughters. It was a moment for soul-talk. Praise, thanksgiving, wonder! It took me days to return to any sense of inner normality, so great was the ecstasy of the disruptive moment.

The earlier mentioned prophet Isaiah traces for us a disruptive moment of wonderment when he recalls a powerful vision of God in the temple. Whether he is describing a dream or a real-time experience, we do not know. But the prophet tells us that in a crisis moment (the death of a powerful king), he has a wonder-filled moment of the glory of God.

You can tell that Isaiah is reaching for language that will approximate what he has experienced. "I saw the LORD, high and lifted up," he writes. And in the following lines he describes a dramatic display (some might call it pyrotechnical) of lights, smoke, angels, sounds. I tell you, the man is struggling to describe the inexplainable. In a word, he is caught up in wonderment.

And his wonderment becomes a disruptive moment. Among the results, apparently, is a first-look inward toward the inner space of his soul where he sees little more than evil that must be named and confessed. And following that, Isaiah is provided with forgiving grace and a chance to hear the voice of God.

Disruptive moments of wonderment do not always have the same results. Jonah had one in the innards of a great fish, and Moses had one in front of a burning bush. They were consumed by the experience and were changed by it. But others were not so impressed, such as some of the spectators who surrounded Jesus and tried to diminish the significance of His miracles with rational explanation.

Not long ago, I took a few days to walk a New Hampshire portion of the Appalachian Trail. I stayed one night at a hikers' hut where thirty people (mostly strangers) can find shelter and then stretch out their sleeping bags for a fitful night's sleep.

The Appalachian Mountain Club, which maintains these shelters, likes to provide a naturalist or two for each of its huts so that the evenings can be filled with interesting lectures about things pertaining to nature (which I prefer to call creation). On this particular night a wife and husband offered two lectures: she a geologist and he an astronomer.

We other twenty-eight tired hikers listened first to the geologist tell us the theories of the origin of the mountains and the drifting continental plates that caused their upsurge. She talked in terms of hundreds of millions of years, gargantuan time spans, and massive glaciers. It was intriguing.

Then the astronomer turned our attention to the heavens. He pointed out planets, stars, constellations, and other heavenly bodies. He spoke of light-years in the tens of thousands. Pointing to one star, he informed us that the light we were seeing had begun its journey in our direction fifteen million years ago. It also was intriguing, and by the end of the evening I was in a wonderment state of soul.

Later approaching the couple to thank them for their talks, I asked "Do you ever have any visceral reactions to your own topics? What goes on within you when you think in terms of these massive time frames and senses of infinity?"

In seconds it became clear that neither had interest in my questions. "I've made a decision not to think about it," the astronomer said. "The facts are simply greater than my mind, and I'll leave it at that."

These are the words of a person who refuses to be disturbed by the signals of wonderment. An old nursery rhyme hints at what it is like to have one's sights set so low that wonderment is lost:

> Pussycat, pussycat, where have you been?
> I've been to London to visit the queen.
> Pussycat, pussycat, what did you see there?
> I saw a little mouse under a chair.

## The Disruptive Moment of Aging:
### *A Process We Cannot Avoid*

If crisis describes an event we cannot control, and if wonderment is a word attached to an event we cannot explain, *aging is a process we cannot avoid.*

I write at a time when I am in my fifties. Younger people think me old; older people envy me—so they say—for my relative youthfulness. I'm sure I've much yet to learn about aging, but I am now well acquainted with the curriculum.

I no longer can take my body for granted; my mind finds it difficult to memorize as easily as it once did. I find myself instinctively resistant to new paradigms or perspectives. I live with the insistent temptation to return to yesterday's values and customs; I am much more comfortable with them.

I perceive myself more and more of a spectator while a younger generation seems to take charge of more and more contemporary events. Enough time has passed for my generation to sort itself out in terms of success, mediocrity, and failure. A few have gone on to one form of greatness or another; a greater percentage seem to have settled for averageness, and we would be content to leave a modest legacy. And a percentage (not for me to estimate) are dropping out here and there. Those of us in this category lie, as it were, at the roadside mourning our lost dreams and aspirations, and we mourn that the journey was all too short. And how shall we live through the aging process, this experience we cannot avoid?

Some will simply do all they can to deny its happening and thus, crazy as it sounds, try to avoid the unavoidable. The avoiders will dye their hair, keep weight down, enter triathlons, wear stylish clothes. Perhaps if they do this—and much more—they can circumvent for a few more years the stark message that life is advancing, even winding down. That one day they too shall face the inevitable—a departure from this life as they've known it into something beyond.

T. S. Eliot in his poem "The Love Song of J. Alfred Prufrock" seems to understand this reflection when he writes,

> I have seen the moment of my greatness flicker,
> And I have seen the eternal Footman hold my
>     coat, and snicker,
> And in short, I was afraid.

I am haunted by the words of the late Joseph Alsop who, in his memoirs, wrote, "The truth is, I could no longer understand what was happening in America, perhaps because I had finally become an old man frozen in the viewpoints of the past."

But here and there the aging process will cause a person to look beneath the waterline. That was the thought of St. Paul when he wrote,

> We do not lose heart. Even though our outward man is perishing, yet the inward man is being renewed day by day. For our light affliction, which is but for a moment, is working for us a far more exceeding and eternal weight of glory, while we do not look at the things which are seen, but at the things which are not seen. For the things which are seen are temporary, but the things which are not seen are eternal (2 Cor. 4:16–18).

I shall have more to say about the aging process later on, but for this moment, it is important to say that the aging-thoughts are themselves a significant disruptive moment or experience. In a world where human life is all there is, aging is frightening. Time moves faster and faster; the scope of one's world tends to lessen; negative feelings, irritations, and fears seem harder to keep secret. For a large part of the senior population, life is not fun.

But what if aging causes one to look more deeply into the soul? What if it is possible to find what eluded a host of naive explorers, an actual fountain of perpetual youthfulness built upon energy that comes from the soul?

It was Malcolm Muggeridge who probably did more than anyone else to alert the world to the extraordinary Mother Teresa. His first writings about her are contained in the small book *Something Beautiful for God.* Of this woman whom God used to bring the gospel into focus for him, he writes, "I never met anyone more memorable. Just meeting her for a fleeting moment, makes an ineffaceable impression." Why? What is it that captures his attention? Remember, this is an aging woman of whom he speaks. He goes on,

> Something of God's universal love has rubbed off on Mother Teresa, giving her homely features a noticeable luminosity; a shining quality. She has lived so closely with her Lord that the same enchantment clings about her that sent the crowds chasing after him in Jerusalem and Galilee, and made his presence seem a harbinger of healing.

As I learn to surrender my external needs to be numbered or admired because I am among the young and powerful, I have found much peace below the waterline. No longer am I overly preoccupied with the competitive pressures of yesterday. No longer must

I prove myself over and over again. No longer am I under pressure to be attractive to everyone. And no longer do I always have to be right, be the first, be in control.

Facing the fact that I have now lived more years than I am probably going to live (or want to live), I am enabled to think more meaningfully about what is really important and Who it is that will make that final determination.

Richard Rohr notes that in India, life is seen in four phases. There is first the phase of the student where one sets out to learn all he can from the wise men. Then there is the phase of the house-holder where one marries, establishes a home and a family, and provides what is needed. A third phase comes in the wake of the householder period, and that is the phase of the seeker. The seeker goes out into the world to learn what is really important in the light of many years of life. The seeker is prepared to listen in humility and is not distracted with the need to prove himself or demonstrate his power.

But there is another phase: the earnest seeker becomes the wise man to whom the students come. The wise man is the one who speaks out of the soul and who has become comfortable with but respectful of the deeper mysteries. One finds peace and wisdom in the presence of the wise person.

And none of this can happen apart from aging.

It is instructive, I think, that among the very first people to give witness to the uniqueness of the Christ child in the arms of Joseph and Mary are Simeon and Anna, two aged people who have become content to leave the marketplace and its frenzy and wait in the temple for the "Consolation of Israel" (Luke 2:25). Not an attractive option for those of us who seek big houses, magnificent cars, and fail-safe financial pictures before we get old. But we envy their contentment as they hold the Christ child in their arms and look heavenward. They know something most of us do not.

# The Disruptive Moment of Spiritual Discipline:
*Something Most of Us Would Rather Not Do*

Crisis: what we cannot control. Wonderment: what we cannot explain. Aging: what we cannot avoid. And now the fourth of these disruptive moments, which moves us inward and downward below the waterline toward soul territory.

*Spiritual disciplines are those things that—more than likely— most of us would rather not do.* Discipline is that act of inducing pain and stress in one's life in order to grow into greater toughness, capacity, endurance, or strength. So spiritual discipline is that effort pressing the soul into greater effort so that it will enlarge its capacity to hear God speak and, as a result, to generate inner force (spiritual energy) that will guide and empower one's mind and outer life.

The fact that we use a word like *discipline* in spiritual matters is probably an admission that life has a tendency to pursue disorderliness and laziness. Thus, we discipline ourselves to avoid this.

Athletes such as the runner, the swimmer, and the wrestler all understand that pain is an indicator that one is crossing the threshold into extraordinary performance. When I was an athlete on the track and cross-country circuit, I don't think I understood this. No one had adequately conveyed to me the notion that pain was the beginning of growth. Thus, I naturally saw pain as the end of growth. When my body began to hurt after a difficult workout, I took it as a signal to quit.

Bill Toomey ranks as one of America's great twentieth-century athletes. He brought the gold medal for the decathlon back to the United States in the 1960s.

I was a member of Bill Toomey's track team at the University of Colorado in the late fifties. We ran side by side (at least for the first fifty yards) in most workouts. To this day I have anguished memories of our workouts each Monday afternoon. The memories are onerous because the workouts were. When those Monday workouts were ended, I would stagger in exhaustion to the locker room.

But not Bill Toomey. He would rest on the grass beside the track for twenty minutes, and then he would repeat the workout. For every ounce of drive I had in me, Bill Toomey had ten more.

And that's why American sports fans knew Bill Toomey's name in the sixties and no one knew or cared about mine. The difference between the two of us began on Monday afternoons during workouts. He was unafraid of discipline and did the maximum; I was afraid of discipline and did the minimum.

Years later I have learned that nothing of value is ever acquired without discipline. And so it is with those issues that exist below the waterline, at soul-level. Here it is that one learns—to use words from Thomas à Kempis—to walk inwardly.

The spiritual masters have taught us this in every possible way. They have warned us that the one who would get in touch with the soul must do so with diligence and determination. One must overcome feelings, fatigue, distractions, errant appetites, and popular opinion. One must not be afraid of silence, of stillness, or of entering the overpowering presence of divinity with a humble spirit.

Of the four disruptive moments that I've listed, spiritual discipline is the one we can bring under daily control. The first two—crisis and wonderment—are often unplanned. Aging is something we know about but usually pretend won't happen. But discipline is something we can choose to embrace on a daily basis. The choice lies in the decision to set aside the necessary time, embrace the habits of the masters, and engage with a waiting God who seeks our communion.

As I wrote earlier in this chapter, if my life is a road map, it will show that most things happened to me on secondary routes.

That those things were, more often than not, unexpected. There were times when I would rather not have stopped or been stopped. But each time there was an opportunity for soul-talk. I learned; I grew; I gained something else to offer.

# QUALITY OF SOUL

*The desperate need today is not for a*
*great number of intelligent people, or*
*gifted people, but for deep people.*
—Richard Foster

A FRIEND HAS spent his adult life in oil and gas exploration. He has been very successful because he knows his business and works hard. But having said that, his last few business years have been tough, and my friend has flirted with bankruptcy because of a hostile economy and declining oil prices.

In fact, he was just about to exit from the oil and gas business when there was a sudden reversal of events. He and his partners decided to launch one final drilling project that was immediately successful. They struck a reservoir of natural gas that exceeded all expectations and offered every indication of high profitability. Surprise! Overnight, the earlier fearful talk of "going belly-up" turned to anticipation of new prosperity.

In the first month of production the well yielded 3.5 million cubic feet of gas per day, a volume great enough to encourage plans to drill a second well into the same reservoir in order to double the rate of production. No one could have been more excited than my friend. He could sense a dramatic turnaround in his business.

Entrepreneur and dreamer that he was, it was time for new plans and new ventures. The dark days seemed to be over.

Unfortunately, the conclusions and anticipation may have been impulsive. Forty-five days into the life of the well, the flow of gas dramatically diminished. From 3.5 million cubic feet a day to 1 million—now not enough to break even and cover the costs of drilling and production.

Result for my friend: deep, deep disappointment. He was tempted to feel more than a little foolish in the company of all his friends and associates with whom he had shared his newfound hopes and dreams. We didn't see things that way, of course, but there was not much we could do to relieve him of his disillusionment.

Now, after I have told this story—and it is an unfinished story at this writing—things may turn out differently. The well just might resume its earlier output, or it might, in fact, turn out to be the frustrating bust that the more recent experience portends. My friend's disappointing experience with his natural gas well turns me back toward the issues of things below the waterline in life. Issues of the soul.

*Some signal questions:* What can I conclude about the quality of my soul and its ability to produce something *beautiful* for God (a phrase borrowed from Malcolm Muggeridge), something *resourceful* for others, and something *stabilizing and life-giving* for me? Is my soul like a well whose output, if sustained, will lead to prosperity of spirit? Or is it like a well that promises much in its initial output but performs just long enough to raise hopes and then offer powerful disappointment? For the person who chooses to organize his or her life about the God of the Bible, this could be one of life's most important questions. A question answered not just once, but many, many times.

The Older Testament relates the story of Lot, nephew to the

holy and noble Abraham, who traveled as part of the extended Abrahamic family. Wherever Abraham went, so did Lot. And whenever Abraham prospered, so did Lot. I can't prove it, but I have this sense that if you would have visited the two men, you would have gone away impressed with both. And you might have been drawn to Lot, the younger, perhaps the more seemingly ambitious and energetic of the two. You and I might have looked upon Lot's success and assumed that we were in the company of a man with a deep soul, a man greatly blessed of his God. Everything about the man dripped of the "gusher" prosperity that my friend's well showed in its first forty-five days.

And we would have been wrong! The proof that they were two distinctly different men at soul-level came after they separated: one to the plain of Sodom and the other to the hill country. If anything, Abraham who headed for the hills became a better man for the parting of the ways. And if anything, Lot who headed for the lush grasses of Sodom became a worse man. His choices, his values, and his direction in life became all too evident; they put him on a course that diverged from the God of Abraham, away from a life where prosperity of spirit could have been a possibility. For Lot, the story ended in deep tragedy.

Lot teaches me some valuable lessons. Again, he is like the well that gushes for forty-five days and then loses its vitality. He looks terrific under the right circumstances and with influential connections; he looks awful under the wrong circumstances and with nefarious connections. He basks in the influences of the moment: spiritual and holy in the company of his uncle Abraham, something less than admirable in the company of the people of Sodom.

As I have pondered the story of Lot and the lesson of a natural gas well's initial promise followed by its sudden loss of productivity, I have been instructed concerning a potential weakness in my own spiritual journey: *the challenge to discern the difference between a developing authentic spirituality (Abraham) and the almost empty promises of spiritual experiences (Lot).*

Spirituality and spiritual experience: they are two different things and must not be mistaken for each other.

These two concepts—*spirituality* and *spiritual experience*—are so enormous that I write with great fear lest I abuse their meaning and confuse an important issue. But I cannot go further in this subject of living out of the soul without addressing them so that I can use the terms in the course of my writing.

### Spirituality

To me, *spirituality*—a word used by all sorts of people friendly *and* unfriendly to Christian faith—suggests all the efforts involved and all the benefits gained when one chooses to organize his or her life around the soul and its innate capacity to commune with God and play host to His Holy Spirit. Thomas a Kempis called this walking inwardly.

Put in other terms, *spirituality is a journey in the company of the Creator in which He is permitted to guide the way, provide the traveling strength, and offer the necessary sustenance in time of fatigue or injury.* Let me try one more description of this elusive term: *spirituality means taking one's cues not from the world around but from the inner world out of which bubbles heavenly discernment, conviction, and decision. It means a soul in which the Spirit of God is invited to dwell.*

The people with whom I grew up refer to spirituality in terms like these: *walking with Christ, being filled with the Spirit,* and *living victoriously or abundantly.* I've heard others describe spirituality as *living in the Presence* or *walking the holy way.*

This term, *spirituality,* covers a lot of ground. It speaks of the inner demeanor of a person; it refers to his or her conduct and character; and it may go as far as describing what a person thinks about charitable service in the name of Jesus. Clearly, *spirituality* is a very big word. But it has everything to do with what is below the waterline in one's life.

In a day when people seek careers, success, psychological wholeness, wealth, and the so-called good life, I sense that the quest for the spirituality I've just defined has dropped off the horizon for the majority. Churches fill with people who claim that they seek a kind of exemplary Christian life. But for the most part, what they are seeking, and what they are willing to sacrifice to get it, suggests that they are prepared to settle for something far less than true spirituality.

Having offered some definitions of spirituality, let me state what spirituality is not. It is not knowing more Bible stories and memorizing more Bible verses than anyone in church school (as I once may have thought as a child). It is not being hyperactive in church activities. And it is not possessing a highly defined doctrinal position regarding biblical issues. Oh, and spirituality is not tied up in being an evangelist, a missionary, a preacher/teacher, or a lay leader in a congregation. These are all noble and praise-worthy ventures, but they are not necessarily tied to whether one lives out of the soul or not.

Anthony Bloom writes of his own understanding of spirituality as he describes how he came alive to life at soul-level. He apparently had reached a point where he saw his soul like my friend sees his disappointing natural gas well. What we might call religious busyness, Bloom refers to as "purposefulness." He writes,

> I began to look for a meaning in life other than what I could find
> through purposefulness. Studying and making oneself useful for
> life didn't convince me at all. All my life up to now had been

concentrated on immediate goals, and suddenly these became empty. *I felt something immensely dramatic inside myself, and everything around me seemed small and meaningless.* (emphasis mine)

Bloom goes on to describe a personal awakening to something greater, deeper, and more resourceful within himself than can be found in one's public world. For Bloom, the beginning of his spirituality came:

While I was reading the beginning of St. Mark's Gospel, before I reached the third chapter . . . I suddenly became aware that on the other side of my desk there was a presence. And the certainty was so strong that it was Christ standing there that it has never left me. This was the real turning point. Because Christ was alive and I had been in his presence I could say with certainty that what the Gospel said about the crucifixion of the Prophet of Galilee was true, and the centurion was right when he said, "Truly he is the Son of God."

This is no small matter of which Bloom speaks. It is challenging, upsetting, surprising, and not a little frightening. And so he goes on,

To meet God means to enter into the "cave of the tiger"—it is not a pussy cat you meet—it's a tiger. The realm of God is dangerous. You must enter into it and not just seek information about it.

You can't read Bloom's description of what happened to him without realizing that something substantial is going on here, something that will mark him for the rest of his life. It is not a cheap and easily generated religious thrill, not a titillation of his feelings. The man will never be the same. This is his conversion, the opening of his soul to Jesus, the living Son of God. And it will ignite a lifelong experience of converting as more and more of his soul is possessed as the dwelling place of God within.

## The Spiritual Experience

Bloom's description of the beginnings of his own spiritual journey is in powerful contrast to what I call the spiritual experience. This latter concept is what some might call a quick fix that is more centered in the emotions or the mind rather than the soul. It is quite possible that, for a moment, a spiritual experience is actually more tranquilizing *or* more stimulating than anything spirituality has to offer. And that's important to understand. To use Bloom's words, entering the cave of the tiger is hardly a tranquilizing experience. Perhaps a spiritual experience might be more attractive.

In a world where the intensity of an experience is of great value, we are easily duped into thinking that a personal momentary religious incident that leaves us ecstatic or astonished is far more genuine and satisfying than the hard work of developing spirituality.

William Butler Yeats describes his version of a spiritual experience:

My fiftieth year had come and gone
I sat a solitary man,
In a crowded London shop,
An open book and empty cup
On a marble table top.

While on the shop and street I gazed
*My body for a moment blazed,*
*And twenty minutes, more or less,*

*It seemed so great my happiness,*
*That I was blessed and could bless.*
(emphasis mine)

Note certain words in the second verse: "for a moment," "blazed," "it seemed," "happiness." Such tentative-sounding words and for such a short duration. "It seemed" that I was blessed and could bless. These are the sensations of someone having a spiritual experience.

Spirituality is like a well that produces and produces and produces with long-term profitability. But a spiritual experience is like the well my friend and his partners seem to have drilled: initial impressive performance (just long enough to be worth talking about) but only short-term viability.

The difference between these two concepts can be further illustrated by an ongoing discussion my wife, Gail, and I have about nutrition. When we arise early in the morning, we tend to go our separate ways in terms of breakfast choices. For years Gail has eaten fruit while I have loitered over a bowl (or two) of my favorite cereal. I won't mention the brand, but I will admit to having enjoyed the same little doughnut-shaped oat cereal for more than fifty years (changes in diet come slowly for me).

My cereal litany remains unchanged over the course of my life. Fill the bowl (the larger the bowl, the better) with as much cereal as it will contain. Pour milk and then spread sugar (the white, processed kind). If no one is looking, add extra sugar. When necessary, add more cereal to finish off the leftover sweetened milk.

Having eaten, I leave the house each morning feeling terrific, and I tell myself that part of the reason—in addition to my wife's good-day kiss—has been my good breakfast.

So then, why am I newly hungry about two hours into the morning? Why do I look impatiently at the clock to see when lunchtime will come? The answer is simple: my enjoyable breakfast cereal with its sugar has done little to give me enduring strength for the day. It has offered only the perception of a satisfying breakfast, but the promise is short-lived. Sugar has let me down with a thud within a short time. Sort of like my friend's gas well.

Gail's fruit carries her throughout the morning, and she never forgets to tell me this. She is not tempted toward a mid-morning snack, and she is not hungry until lunch when she is likely to eat more fruit and a few vegetables.

This breakfast experience is a further picture of spiritual experiences and spirituality. Gail has opted for nutrition; I have chosen taste. And I know she's made the correct choice because I have slowly converted in her direction (with occasional relapses) and find a marked difference in the energy and vitality of my morning.

My early journey of faith was guided by many who mistakenly saw spiritual experiences as the evidence that God was at work in a person's life. Thus, it became important to them to do everything within their power to arouse dramatic experiences of apparent renewal or personal revival. And I suspect that it was sometimes important for me to produce spiritual experiences so that I could please them as well as authenticate myself.

No example is more compelling to me than what used to happen at summer camp and on occasional youth retreats where teenagers spent three or four days together under the guidance of counselors pining for signs that God was at work in young lives.

These events invariably occurred on the last evening. It started as a fireside event at which there was a lot of singing and a devotional talk that always challenged the listener to repent, make things right with God, and offer promises about changes in the future. That was usually followed by what were called testimonies.

In a day unlike today, those testimony times were called, strangely enough, faggot services, named for small strips of wood (faggots), the tips of which were soaked in kerosene so that they would burn easily when touched by fire. Even the assistance of kerosene so that the faggot would burn bright and long was symbolic of the quick fix our lives were supposed to experience at the fire in the moonlight. But I didn't see that then.

We teens were challenged to leave our places and approach the fire, grab a faggot, and set it burning while we told the crowd of our intentions to live a more faithful Christian life in future days. Often our statements sounded something like this:

> I've not been much of a Christian during the last year. I've run with the wrong crowd, done some stupid stuff, and pretty much let the Lord down.

At this point the speaker (boy or girl) often fell into a tearful state and after some stifled sobs of remorse would continue:

> But this year things are going to be different. I've decided to rededicate my life to Christ. I'm going back to witness to all of my friends. My school is going to be a different place because Jesus and I are going to change it. You guys have got to pray for me because it's going to be rough. But with His help, I'm going to do it.

With that the speaker would throw the burning faggot on the fire and return to his or her seat. If the testimony giver had been an infamous juvenile "renegade" the past year, the volume of tears would increase all the more. Counselors and youth leaders would nod to one another and agree that something unique was happening. It would indeed be, everyone predicted, a different year.

I am not ridiculing what we did at those campfire meetings because my recollection is that we all made those fireside declarations in great sincerity. We really did intend to do the things we said. And most of us did . . . for about three days. Some lasted longer.

But after three days, in most cases, it was back to life as usual. The important thing I'm trying to observe is this: *what most of us had during those evenings about the fire (and there were some genuine exceptions) were spiritual experiences and little else.*

Now this is the time to pause in my description of *spiritual experiences* and do my very best to assure that I am properly understood.

By putting the terms *spirituality* and *spiritual experience* in contrast to one another, I am not wanting to raise suspicion about those wonderful moments when one discovers strong emotion while on the spiritual journey. My own experiences with tears, unrestrained joy and laughter, and profound feelings of awe and deep mystery are many. In fact, if these were missing, I would be among the first to wonder if anything else is genuine.

The Bible is filled with examples of men and women who "let it all hang out" as they exalted the One who is God above all gods. They felt impelled to dance, raise hands, weep, stand in deep silence, and shout. Perhaps they were far more emotional than most of us.

No, the issue is not whether we feel or express emotion in this life that comes out of the soul. Rather, the thing that sets my term *spirituality* apart from what I am calling *spiritual experience* is the discovery that emotional displays and sensations are all that there are in one's encounter with heaven. As this chapter continues, therefore, remember that *spiritual experiences* is being used to describe events that do not point to strong souls. At first these events may appear to lead in that direction, but the chances are that they do not.

Spiritual experiences—the kind about which I am expressing caution—tend to center on three perceptions. They can reflect, *first* of all, powerful feelings of regret we have about something that has or has not happened in our past. Or *second,* spiritual experiences can build upon profound feelings of ecstasy we have about the present: often stirred up by music, a persuasive talk, a sense of camaraderie with a group of people, or a theme of shock about something terrible that has happened. *Finally,* spiritual experiences can occur as we are drawn to some great feeling of resolve or intention about the future.

Simon Peter appears to illustrate the third of these perceptions on the night of the Last Supper when he pledges that he will take his place beside Jesus no matter what may occur. He will fight for Him, he promises; he will gladly die for Him. But Jesus knows the soul of Peter well enough to reject this euphoric guarantee and says so. It is as if Jesus says, "You may feel this way now [spiritual experience], but the fact is that when the crunch comes, you will deny Me [due to an inadequate spirituality]."

As I have recounted my own spiritual journey and those frequent occasions of spiritual experience that remind me of disappointing gas wells and sugar highs, I've come to observe these somewhat disenchanting characteristics. They have all come from my personal history.

*First, spiritual experiences require little discipline of the soul.* Because they are usually prompted by an external stimulus (music, persuasive speaking, intense feelings), they can happen at any time, and the person involved need not have prepared himself or herself in any particular way. It is quite possible that the spiritual experience will never reach deep enough into one's life to engage the soul at all.

One can have a spiritual experience with little or no warning. Just create the right kind of outward circumstance, and it can happen. Each year on Palm Sunday the Christian community is reminded of the crowd of well-wishers who waved palms in the face of Jesus and gave Him the praises due a king. There is every indication that the people were caught up in something of a spiritual experience. They would have done anything for Him at that moment—perhaps even gone to their deaths.

Jesus was notably unimpressed with their exaltation. As it says in other parts of the Scripture, "He knew what was in them." Meaning that He heard words and saw gestures, but He knew the souls of people in the particular crowd were empty. And He wouldn't play their game.

Their praise was not the adoration of the prepared soul that generates convictions about who the Son of God really is. Rather, it was the superficial applause of people caught up in mob arousal. Nothing else! And it quickly dissipated—like my friend's well. Spiritual experiences are like that.

*Second, spiritual experiences are almost always a matter of emotion more·than anything else.* There can be tears, laughter, passions of regret or enthusiasm, or senses of powerful love or desire to take great risks.

I remember having something similar to a spiritual experience a few years ago when pop singer Whitney Houston sang the national anthem of the United States at a football game. She sang with such utter abandonment and enthusiasm that tears were freely flowing down my cheeks before she finished. The music had triggered my emotions and loosened their energy. I was momentarily thrilled to be an American.

But it wasn't long after that I was back to feeling ill toward Congress for raising my taxes, toward the president for mismanaging the environment, and toward the Supreme Court for making a wrong judgment on a case I'd followed. It wasn't long until I was ashamed of the neglect of our cities, our abuse of the soil and forest, our cynical treatment of poor nations.

Whitney Houston did not make me a better American. She

provoked an emotional experience. As in Yeats's words, she made me feel happy for twenty minutes, "more or less," that I was blessed and could bless.

I have already illustrated *the third characteristic of a spiritual experience: that it usually lasts for only a short while*. My friend's gas well seems to have been good for only a month. Most spiritual experiences do not last that long.

I have tended to see Simon Peter's attempt to walk toward Jesus on the water as illustrative of a spiritual experience: "Let me do this exciting thing," he seems to be saying. And Jesus permits the moment because it will later teach Simon that there are other things more important than just these attention-riveting miracles that are supposed to daub the soul with so much pleasure.

So Simon begins his walk, and every storyteller in Christian history has imagined how proud he was of himself . . . until he looked down. And he sank! The experience was ended.

Like the results of a breakfast cereal decorated with sugar, the spiritual experience lasts for only a while because it does not emerge from the deeper parts of the soul.

*A fourth characteristic of a spiritual experience is that it tends to bring a perverse honor or exaltation to the actor in the experience*. If man's chief end—as the catechism proposes—is to glorify God, a spiritual experience tends to thwart that. The words may sound authentic, the gestures sublime, but self is usually front and center both internally and externally in the venture. And the spiritual masters have been blunt about this: when self is exalted, God is not present.

Some have been given the privilege of ministry in very public forums—preaching, musical activity, teaching, writing, to name a few. The wisest of them know something of the supreme danger that comes in such undertakings when they are recipients of praise and appreciation from well-meaning people. The applause often contains a false message: that they are God's instruments, regardless of whether they live out of the soul or not, and that they are indispensable to everyone's need.

Leaders can easily be tempted, as a result, to perceive themselves as highly spiritual people when, in fact, they are merely jumping from one spiritual experience to another. In such a context it is not unusual to face enormous inner and outer temptations to various forms of sin. The temptations can center on sexual issues, pride, abuse of power, or recklessness with truth.

One of my great preaching heroes, Alexander Whyte of nineteenth-century Scotland, was approached one day by a woman who showered him with words of praise and flattery. She was sincere, and Whyte knew that. But he also knew that the applause she was heaping upon him was not his to receive, nor was it an accurate perception of what he knew himself to be.

In a response that is more typical of the nineteenth century than the twentieth, he said to her, "Madam, if you knew the man I really was, you would spit in my face." I don't find this response useful in my world, but I think I understand exactly what Alexander Whyte was driving at.

When I think about the propensity of spiritual experiences to exalt the person in an unnatural way, I think about the temptation we all face to talk too much about what we are experiencing. I could be wrong about this, but one of the litmus tests I find myself using to distinguish between growth in spirituality and a spiritual experience is whether or not I have to talk about it and gain the approval or the applause of others.

Men and women of deep souls, who have weight below the waterline, do not need to talk about life at soul-level. It becomes a healthy secret between them and God. The evidence that such life is going on will be seen at stormtime when they ride out the waves while others are capsizing. "Mary kept all these things and pondered them in her heart" (Luke 2:19)—these are the words of one who doesn't need to tell everyone what is happening at soul-level.

Several other characteristics appear to come in the aftermath of spiritual experiences.

I'm thinking of the fact that *spiritual experiences often leave one empty and tired in the end*. I'm back to my story of breakfast cereal. Great start; poor finish.

Perhaps this is something of what happened to the disciples when they walked to the Garden of Gethsemane with the Lord on the night before He was crucified. The time together with Him in the Upper Room had not reached to the depth of their souls (as it would later when they reflected upon what happened). It had all been little more than experience to them. They were confused, not a little scared, and very tired.

When a deeper spirituality would have called them to prayer in the company of the Lord, they chose rather to sleep. And their sleep set them up for a deep descent into defeat when the temple guards came to take Jesus away. Peter drew a sword when he'd been taught for almost three years that you don't draw swords; the disciples ran when they'd been challenged for almost three years to stand their ground and draw strength and speech from God. Some performance! Close the Bible at that point, and you have a bunch of losers and a very embarrassed Jesus.

Emptiness and fatigue are often the threshold to further vulnerability to temptation and sin. There is a blindness that often comes in the wake of spiritual experiences, the result of a rationale that says I have experienced God's presence and felt His power. Nothing can go wrong. That's when the words of St. Paul spring into force: "Let him who thinks he stands take heed lest he fall" (1 Cor. 10:12). And the disciples—despite Jesus' cautions—didn't know that. Were it not for the grace of Jesus that caused Him to go looking for them, I don't know that they would ever have recovered from the failure of that night.

Spiritual experiences have two other possible characteristics. *One of the two is that they often leave us cynical and later resistant to any genuine approach by God's holy presence.* After we have felt let down one too many times, we become increasingly reluctant to go this route again. Perhaps that is not so bad, except that it makes us reluctant to even pursue the genuine article: what I simply call spirituality.

After a half dozen faggot services, I know that I became impervious to the most passionate invitations of Bible teachers. I became a silent spectator and even felt harsh toward those who made their way to speak at the fire. I convinced myself that it was all an act with little value. And it was more than a few years before I could bring myself to become vulnerable again before a group of people when it came to talking about matters of the soul.

*Can I suggest that most spiritual experiences tend to make people look foolish and unreliable?* Over a period of time, such people give the impression of being yo-yos: up and down, back and forth. They are impressive in the moment—as was Peter on the water—but they appear childish in the long run.

I fear that much of what we see on religious television both on the stage and in the audience is little more than spiritual experience. And one wonders what many people look like when the klieg lights dim. The high-pitched enthusiasm, the shrill of hyperactive noise simply cannot be sustained. Sooner or later, one has to come down to something that looks like normal. And when that happens, the spiritual experience is over, and the soul remains unconvinced.

Having observed all of this, it may be important to backtrack just a bit and say that events that come under the description of spiritual experience may indeed lead to something deeper and beneficial to the soul. Although there have been many disappointing spiritual experiences, one does come to a moment that is more than experience. Suddenly, there is an explosion of insight, and the hunger to go beyond the initial experience becomes all-consuming.

John Wesley's experience at Aldersgate became the ignition of his great conversion to Jesus Christ. Charles Colson's moment of deep despair in which he cries out to God while seated in his car, "Take me, take me," is an experience on its way to becoming great spirituality. But these experiences were quickly followed up and deepened. They were not, as in the parable Jesus told, seeds that took root in shallow soil, grew up among thorns, or lay vulnerable to the hungry birds.

When a small boy, I was romanced, as were so many others my age, with the thrice-weekly adventures of the Lone Ranger on the radio. The thrilling stories "from out of the pages of yesteryear" of the "masked rider of the plains" and his "faithful Indian companion, Tonto," were an inspiration to me. My greatest wish was that I could be like him, and that I could someday save a town held hostage by the bad guys or that I could rescue some lovely woman whose ranch was being threatened by a crooked banker. I dreamed of such an opportunity.

And such an opportunity did, in fact, come. On the streets of St. Louis one evening as I stood in line to purchase theater tickets, I heard the scream of a woman in distress down the block from where I stood. Almost instantly I saw a person (man or woman I could not tell) running in my direction, a purse in the hand. The scream and the running figure suggested purse snatching.

I had the space of about two seconds to decide on a course of action. The Lone Ranger would have thrown himself into the fleeing figure, a body block that would have sent the thief flying. I could do that perhaps. Maybe he would have drawn his gun and intimidated the robber into stopping. But what was I to do? I had just a second now as he ran toward me.

Did anyone ever sue the Lone Ranger for false arrest? I thought about that. Did the Lone Ranger ever discover that when he needed his gun, he'd forgotten it on the front seat of his car? I wondered about that since I didn't have a weapon. Did the Lone Ranger ever worry about his health insurance being invalid in cases of body blocks being thrown in the name of law and order? That crossed my mind. And now I had just a half of a second to know what I would do. The thief was almost an arm's length away.

I'll tell you what I did. Nothing! Nothing! I just let him run right by while I kept on thinking. All the Lone Ranger stories had not done an ounce of good. Being a hero was a wonderful concept when it was on the radio and in the mind. But on the streets of St. Louis, it was another matter. Too many complicating possibilities.

And I thought of the difference between Simon Peter's enthusiastic assurance in the Upper Room, a very safe place, that he would be the hero and the complicating possibilities there in the Garden of Gethsemane. Suddenly, hero behavior wasn't very attractive. For in Simon's case and in mine, our conviction that we were bred to be heroes wasn't yet at soul-level.

The truth? Both of us were like my friend's well: forty-five days of profitable gas, not much else. And that's spiritual experience.

# QUESTING FOR SPIRITUALITY

*'Twas August and the fierce sun overhead*
*Smote on the squalid slums of Bethnal Green,*
*And the pale weaver, through his window seen*
*In Spitalfields, look'd thrice dispirited.*

*I met a preacher there I knew, and said:*
*'Ill and o'erworked, how fare you in this scene?'*
*'Bravely,' said he, 'for I of late have been*
*Much cheer'd with thoughts of Christ, the living bread.'*
—Matthew Arnold

SPIRITUALITY IS QUITE different. You know it when you see it in the life of a longtime saint. Take William Booth, founder (with his wife, Catherine) of the Salvation Army. One of his biographers tells of the day when the general was in his eighties. He was ill and had been to see a physician. It was left to his son, Bramwell, to tell him that he would soon be blind.

"You mean that I am going blind?"

"Well, General, I fear that we must contemplate that," said Bramwell, who along with the family had always addressed their father by that affectionate name.

There was a pause while Booth thought over what he had been told.

And then the father asked the son, "I shall never see your face again?"

"No, probably not in this world," was the son's reply.

The biographer writes,

During the next few moments the veteran's hand crept along the counterpane to take hold of his son's, and holding it he said very calmly, "God must know best!" And after another pause, "Bramwell, I have done what I could for God and for the people with my eyes. Now I shall do what I can for God and for the people without my eyes."

This is the evidence of spirituality.

Jesus was thinking of spirituality when He reiterated the great commandment: "You shall love the LORD your God with all your heart, with all your soul, with all your mind, and with all your strength" (Mark 12:30). And St. Paul was thinking of spirituality when he challenged the Roman Christians to "be transformed by the renewing of your mind" (Rom. 12:2).

What might a person of deep spirituality look like? We've already seen a page from William Booth's life. Let me take another, more modern personality.

Recently, I was thumbing through a biography of Robert Speer, a leader in the worldwide missions movement in the early part of the twentieth century. Speer has been for many a somewhat controversial figure, but all who knew him seemed to agree on one thing: he had a deep and abiding spirituality.

Emile Calliet, writing many years ago, wrote of the impression Speer made upon him:

When I was on the faculty of the graduate school of the University of Pennsylvania, I was invited every year to lecture at the Princeton Institute of Theology. Like every other visiting professor, I lived at the Princeton Inn. Every morning the activities of the day were opened at the Princeton Theological Seminary by a Bible Hour of which Dr. Speer was in charge. He would get up, have an early breakfast, and although my lecture came much later, I made it a point of getting up so as to sit at the breakfast table with him. If there was anyone who did not need to prepare it was Dr. Speer; and yet I never saw anyone prepare more carefully. Even through out the breakfast, after the usual kind word of welcome and friendly inquiries, he would remain silent. I respected his silence because I knew it was that of an active meditation on his coming Bible Hour. So you may ask why did I sit at the table with him at all. The answer is: just to be with him and look at him. He was a Presence. It was good to be there.

After the Institute was over, I would come back to Philadelphia, and often my wife would exclaim, "Why there is a light on your face!" And I would merely answer, "I spent a few days with Robert Speer." (Speer, p. 280)

As I read these words, I found myself pondering a question I'd not asked often enough: Where are those people whose spirituality, whose inward connection with God, is so evident that others are caused to want to just look at them?

My grandfather, Thomas MacDonald, was one of them. He was a civil engineer who walked away from a promising career because teaching the Bible became more important to him than building bridges. My grandfather was a gentle, quiet-spoken man, and the orbits of our lives did not offer enough opportunity for me to know him as well as I now wish.

As a small boy, I saw him often seated in a large chair in his office with an open Bible—always an open Bible—on the table before him. He would pore over it for hours and then teach its contents to student missionaries. How he loved the Bible! His engineer's instinct for thoroughness transferred to his Bible exploration and teaching. Nothing was left to guesswork.

Grandfather MacDonald was passionate about a few things. One of them was prayer. He loved God, loved God's work, and loved anyone who was committed to evangelism. It was because of his challenge to me when I was a boy that I have had an affection for the northeastern part of North America all of my life. "If God ever permits you to be a preacher of the gospel," he would say to me, "come and do your preaching in the Northeast. That's where you'll be needed most."

When my grandfather was a very old man, he spent his final year in a home for retired people in Quarryville, Pennsylvania. I went to see him on a couple of occasions. Visits were difficult because his mind was virtually gone, and he operated mostly on instinct alone. But the gentle, noble spirit was always there. And it was there the day I went to see him for the last time.

"Grandfather, I'm Gordon," I said when I sat down beside his chair, feeling foolish that I, his grandson, was having to introduce myself. But he had no memory for names or people any longer.

"Who are you?" he asked in spite of my introduction.

"I'm Gordon, Donald's son." But it made no difference. He didn't remember.

So I simply told him what I'd come to say. "Grandfather, I want you to know that I did go back to the Northeast. I'm a pastor now of a wonderful congregation of people in Massachusetts. I preach the Bible to them every week. Your prayers for me are answered." I told him that he had two great-grandchildren, that they were full of life and promise. That I had a wonderful wife; that I was a very happy man.

"Oh, that's so good," he responded, still not sure of who I was. I think he was being kind since that was the only thing he knew to do all of his life.

When it came time to leave him, I said, "Grandfather, I'd like to pray for you." He was delighted. I began to pray the best prayer I knew how to pray. I prayed for his health, for God to be present to him, for him to remember that he was loved by his family.

And when I finished, I looked up to say good-bye. But it was clear that Grandfather had no intention of saying farewell yet. He was going to pray also.

And pray he did. Suddenly, a foggy mind cleared. And words of praise and intercession poured from his lips, an articulate prayer if I have ever heard one. I was awestruck. The old man: now incontinent in his physical frailty, oblivious of the world beyond the door, unable even to remember his grandson's name. But he knew God, and he knew how to talk with Him. I listened on, and the minutes passed by as he spoke of great biblical promises, as he challenged God to show mercy on a broken world, as he expressed thanksgiving for the love of Jesus. And then it was clear that he was going to pray also for me.

"And now, O God, I pray for . . . [then to me] what is your name?"

"Gordon," I said.

"Yes, thank you." And the prayer continued, ". . . for Gordon that You would bring upon him a heavy anointing of the prophet's power when he preaches the gospel. And, O God, would You give . . . [again, to me] what is your name again?"

"Gordon," I said again.

". . . give Gordon a double measure of blessing as he . . ." And the prayer for me went on with four or five further reminders of my name.

My grandfather knew nothing else, needed to know nothing else, really, except how to live out of the soul. No senility in that dimension of his life. Only beauty, order, truth, power, and glory!

Where are the men and women like him? The "deep people," Richard Foster calls them.

Of course deep people can experience backlashes that are unpredictable. Calliet wanted to be at breakfast with Robert Speer just to look at him. When, as recorded in the Bible, certain religious leaders looked at Stephen and saw a man with the face of an angel, they went ballistic (as we now say) and stoned him to death. Spirituality has its price.

Unlike so many things in our age, genuine spirituality is, more often than not, going to be seen in older rather than younger people. The media will glamorize the young and beautiful woman, the talented male athlete in his twenties, or the younger man or woman who has blazed a successful pathway in the world of the professions. But youth will rarely be found among the ranks of people possessing great spirituality.

I make this observation not to discourage the younger person but to point out that spirituality is something that demands time and experience to develop. It is not found at a weekend retreat or after a year of seminary. Spirituality occurs as an accumulation of years of routine experiences and crisis moments. In fact, the growth of the soul is usually so slow that it is hardly measurable or visible. This is a perfect reason why many Western Christians are not marked with, as Calliet called it, the Presence. They do not have the patience that spiritual development requires.

There is the story of a learned man who came to visit a rebbe. The scholar was no longer a young man—he was close to 30—but he had never before visited a rebbe.

"What have you done all your life?" the master asked him.

"I have gone through the whole of the Talmud three times," answered the learned man.

"Yes, but how much of the Talmud has gone through you?" the rebbe inquired.

Another thing that makes spirituality a rare commodity in our presence is the fact that it is often forged in the context of silence and submission, two experiences that most of us have been taught to avoid whenever possible.

The almost demonic spirit of noise that has filled the air about our lives is a surefire guarantee that most people will never inquire of their souls.

The soul needs its silent spaces, writes Samuel Chadwick:

It is in them we learn to pray. There, alone, shut in with God, our Lord bids us pray to our Father who is in secret, and seeth in secret. There is no test like solitude. . . . The heart shrinks from being alone with God. . . . It would revolutionize the lives of most [people] if they were shut in with God in some secret place for half an hour a day.

As I write the early draft of this chapter, I am at our New Hampshire retreat, which for these past sixteen years we have called Peace Ledge. Gail and I are asked occasionally how we came to call this old New England farm by such a name. The word *ledge* came about because our land—like most of New England—is little more than a bed of rock covered by six inches of not-so-good topsoil.

The word *peace* came about because there is something about this place that smacks of peace. People whose lives were in great turmoil have often come to this place at our invitation. They have come exhausted, in despair, in defeat or failure, with spiritual emptiness. And something has happened to them in this place. Just as it always seems to happen to us. Peace has descended upon them. Restoration has happened: grace, inner and outer strength, reconciliation with God, with themselves.

Soon after we had built our saltbox cape home, Gail came across a lovely poem written by Ruth Bell Graham in which she spoke of a place on the Graham property in Montreat, North Carolina, where she often went in search of quiet. She described her place poetically:

This is my ledge
of quiet
my shelf of peace,
edged
by its crooked rails
holding back the beyond.
Above,
a hawk sails high
to challenge clouds
trespassing
my plot of sky.
Below
in the valley,
remote and dim,
sounds
come and go,
a requiem
for quiet.
Here on my ledge,
quiet praise,
of birds,
crickets,
breeze—
in different ways;
and so do I—
for these;
my ledge of quiet,
my plot of sky;
for peace.

When Gail brought me a copy of the poem and said that it described her experience here at our New Hampshire home, we knew we had a name: *Peace Ledge*. Today if you enter our country home by the front door, the first thing you see is Mrs. Graham's poem, framed, hanging on the wall in the entranceway.

I tell you all of that because this is the place where we have found our silence. Peace Ledge is the place to which we fled when we knew the darkest hours of life; the place where our children and now our grandchildren have known the vitality of deep family experiences; the place where we have come to study, to refresh our souls, to find new strength. And the thing that most marks this place apart from its simple New Hampshire beauty is the silence. The silence! A silence broken only by creation's natural sounds: birds, crickets, chattering chipmunks, and the breeze charging through the forest.

I found myself asking just a day or two ago why it was that a few weeks here always seemed to change my entire sense of life's priorities, my closeness to God, my love of simple things. And then the insight hit me—why there are so few in whom the Presence is sensed. It takes a life lived more in the context of silence than noise to produce such a spirituality. Noise has intruded itself far beyond our ears and has reached the level of the soul and has polluted that part of us as surely as acid rain pressed into the sky from the Ohio River Valley has polluted the forests of New England and the eastern provinces of Canada.

In part, one of the reasons we have to look backward in history to find great saints with enviable spirituality is that their lives were lived with great dosages of silence. And in the silences God found easy freedom to whisper His promises and His purposes into the synapses of the soul.

Thomas Kelley writes,

We feel honestly the pull of many obligations and try to fulfill them all. And we are unhappy, uneasy, strained, oppressed, and fearful we shall be shallow. . . . We have hints that there is a way of life vastly richer and deeper than all this hurried existence, a life of unhurried serenity and peace and power. If only we could slip over into that center. We have seen and known some people who have found this deep Center of living, where the fretful calls of life are integrated, where NO as well as YES can be said with confidence.

Please, don't forget the word I linked with silence, and that is the word *submission*. The choice (about which I shall speak more later on) to enter into covenant with another person(s) for the purposes of community and guidance.

Those in the tradition of the spiritual masters have known something for centuries that we in my tradition greatly misunderstand. And that is that no one can journey alone—much less grow—in the pursuit of spirituality. Everyone must be submitted to someone in a relationship where there is freedom to ask questions that penetrate to the soul and examine values, choices, motives, and affections.

But we Westerners—especially we Americans—are an independent sort. We have been inculturated with the notion of the solo performer, the individual who can handle his or her own affairs and needs no one. And I am blunt to say, and will try to say more forcefully later on, that people cannot hope to possess spirituality if they seek to avoid that covenantal relationship called submission.

As we continue to list some of the characteristics of spirituality, it is important to note that we are questing for something that is often scorned by onlookers, is unappreciated by culture, and will garner little, if any, praise from one's peers.

I am speaking of the larger society of which we are all a part. Spirituality is simply not a value in our day. Spirituality does not guarantee jobs; it does not pave the way for invitations to join a country club; and it usually gets no notice in society columns or on TV magazine shows. In fact, spirituality as a quality of life may even be confused with personality weakness, and those bent on a lifestyle that expunges all things divine may even find themselves uncomfortable in the company of a person marked with spirituality. They will not understand their own feelings, but most likely the inner life will be repelled like a magnet is repelled by another when similar poles are touched. They may feel at the deepest levels a sense of rebuke, conviction, and unsettledness. And they will want out!

May I go on to observe that spirituality is not based upon one's ability to manage knowledge or one's possession of an engaging personality? Some of those who have walked inwardly have been among the simplest of people and have not found it necessary to find a place at the top levels of the personality hit parade.

The pursuit of spirituality also heightens the probability of two other things that most of us find rather unpopular: the pain of self-discovery and often humiliation.

Self-discovery in soul-development means renunciation of the claims of ego. And this is no easy battle for any of us. As we seek the enlargement of that inner place where God may be heard, there is the inevitable discovery of attitudes and desires that are inimical to the holy way. They cannot be rationalized, excused, or denied; they must be named or confessed, renounced, replaced. And none of this is necessarily a pleasant experience.

One winter weekend we had a sewage problem in our septic system at Peace Ledge. Workmen had to dig up a portion of our backyard where the tank holding sewage was located. I cannot do justice with words to the sight and the smell that greeted us as the tank's lid was raised. That was one time I was pleased to be paying someone else to do a job.

As I stood at the side of the hole cheering on the workmen, I could not avoid the temptation to see one more illustration of what happens when one journeys into inner space toward the soul. The beautiful sod is removed and the digging begins. And when the lid comes off, many of the discoveries are simply not pleasant.

No wonder St. Paul, who had spent the large part of his early life keeping the lid to his soul nailed down, cried out with sorrow when he thought of what was deep within: "O wretched man that I am! Who will deliver me from this body of death?" (Rom. 7:24).

I can only speculate on some things, but I am aware that many of the spiritual masters felt that the soul had a dimension of infinite darkness that contained not only an accumulation of sins and foul attitudes from a lifetime but the residue of past generations visited upon us. The passions, the lusts, the angers from the past: down in the sewage of our souls. They, too, must be faced, named, and brought into the light for a redeeming God to bring to healing.

In the biblical passages, I see various men and women who went through many of these processes, and I am impressed with their responses when the pressure rises.

There are Paul and Silas, badly beaten and thrown into prison without defense. They sing and worship late into the night. What leads men in such threatening conditions to act so?

There is the aforementioned Stephen, pelted with bone-crushing and life-ending stones, kneeling and praying for the forgiveness of his enemies. Daniel on his knees—three times a day—facing Jerusalem as he seeks the wisdom of his God. Or Esther who coils up her courage and enters into supreme danger in order to save her people from a holocaust. Moses, who stands alone at the shore of the Red Sea, and says to his people, "Stand still and wait to see what God will do."

Where do such folk come from? They come from the ranks of those who saw that spiritual experience alone offered nothing of substance. From those who understood, to quote Teilhard de Chardin, that "we are not human beings having a spiritual experience but spiritual beings having a human experience." For them, encountering the God who meets men and women at soul-level was more important than anything else.

Joan Chittester reaches into the literature of the monastics to remember a time when a great army invaded a country and created a path of destruction wherever they went. Their greatest wrath was reserved for the holy people they found, particularly the monks. Chittester writes,

> When the invaders arrived in one of the villages . . . the leader of the village reported to the commander, "All the monks, hearing of your approach, fled to the mountains."
>
> The commander smiled a broad, cold smile, for he was proud of having a reputation for being a very fearsome person.
>
> But then the leader added, "All, that is, but one."
>
> The commander became enraged. He marched to the monastery and kicked in the gate. There in the courtyard stood the one remaining monastic. The commander glowered at the figure. "Do you know who I am?" the commander demanded. "I am he who can run you through with a sword without batting an eyelash."
>
> And the monastic fixed the commander with a serene and patient look and said, "And do you know who I am? I am one who can let you run me through with a sword without batting an eyelash."
>
> (Chittester. *Wisdom from the Daily*, p. 184)

The story is old and undocumented, perhaps nothing more than a legend. But it describes the mark of spirituality. One hears of people like this and knows that they have never been content with the sugar of experiences alone. Real or fictional, this monk is an accurate picture of one who lives out of the soul.

# THE STARE OF THE SNAKE

*I took the [road] less traveled by,*
*And that has made all the difference.*
—Robert Frost

IN A THOUGHTFUL book on spiritual life, Carlos Villas, a Spanish monk who has lived much of his life in India, tells of a bicycle ride and a strange experience in the Indian countryside. He had become aware, he writes, of an unusual silence in which all the normal noises and motions of nature seemed to come to a halt. At first there was no discernible explanation, and he was puzzled.

But then, Villas says, he saw something off to one side, and the mystery became clear. There, not far from where the monk stood with his bicycle, was a snake, its head slowly bobbing and weaving as it fixed upon a small bird perched on a lower branch of a shrub. The bird seemed paralyzed, as if locked in a hypnotic trance, by the snake's motions. It appeared incapable of flight.

Villas braced in anticipation of the snake's strike, wondering at the same time if there was something he could do to save the ill-fated bird. Then knowing no other alternative, he attempted to distract the snake by rushing toward it, waving his arms and shouting loudly. Perhaps his actions would also arouse the bird from its seeming stupor.

The effort was successful. The snake's arresting stare was broken, and the bird—free of the "hypnosis"—instantly spread its wings and leaped skyward.

When I read Carlos Villas's account of the moment, I gained a bit of insight into a much more tragic issue: the picture of the spiritual captivity of the human being, the difficulty of living out of a soul highly influenced by the issues of evil.

No inventory of the waterline issues would be useful if it did not take the matter of evil—its power and its consequences—into account and finally ask the question: How, in the human experience, is the stare of the snake broken? Who has the power to break it? And what does the flight of a liberated one look like?

The stare of the snake is a major theme from one end of holy Scripture to another. The human condition is variously described in terms of being held hostage, caught in a kind of slavery, being hopelessly lost in strange territory, and being ravaged by a terminal disease. There are other equally unpleasant likenesses. But in each case the biblical writers are straining to describe the awful injury to the human spirit that has reduced humanity from the once beautiful position of being in the likeness of God's character and personhood to one of being of barbarian quality.

Clearly, the biblical view of humanity's condition is not a complimentary one, and this makes "enlightened" people uncomfortable with, even hostile to, Scripture. But there are only two sources for evil that we can look at. One is the external world in which we live with all of its accumulated influences. The other is the human soul, that spiritual source deep within every person. Jesus made it plain that the latter, not the former, explained the corruption of human behavior and relationship:

For out of the heart proceed evil thoughts, murders, adulteries, fornications, thefts, false witness, blasphemies. These are the things which defile a man, but to eat with unwashed hands does not defile a man (Matt. 15:19–20).

The Bible does not take this position simplistically. It does not bad-mouth humanity, as some people think. Rather, it begins by describing the inestimable beauty of humankind. Its original descriptions of the person paint men and women as being made in God's own image and enjoying the supreme position in all of creation. The ultimate purpose of the first man and the first woman was to reflect the glory of God and engage in intimate union with Him. We can only speculate on what that must have been like, but I cannot help imagining that the ability of the first man and the first woman to think, discover, communicate, and labor together must have been far, far beyond anything we know today.

But almost all of this, the Bible informs, was forfeited in a subsequent set of events that set aside the original purposes. The account of the original act of disobedience is the seedbed for all rebellious behavior today. Frank Sinatra's rendition of "I Did it My Way" becomes the theme song of all those who prefer the divergent path away from the Creator. The song sounds brave and admirable, but it is only a small part of the story.

A. W. Tozer reflected on this struggle below the waterline like this:

> The deep disease of the human heart is a will broken loose from its center, like a planet which has left its central sun and started to revolve around some strange body from outer space which may have moved in close enough to draw it away.

And Dorothy Sayers writing more than fifty years ago vividly commented on the stare-of-the-snake condition:

A young and intelligent priest remarked to me the other day that he thought one of the greatest sources of strength in Christianity today lay in the profoundly pessimistic view it took of human nature. There is a great deal in what he says. The people who are most discouraged and made despondent by the barbarity and stupidity of human behavior at this time are those who think highly of Homo Sapiens as a product of evolution and who still cling to the optimistic belief in the civilizing influence of progress and enlightenment. To them the appalling outbursts of bestial ferocity in the totalitarian states, and the obstinate selfishness of capitalist society, are not merely shocking and alarming. For them, these things are the utter antithesis of everything in which they have believed. The whole thing looks like a denial of all reason, and they feel as if they and the whole world had gone mad together.

Now for the Christian this is not so. He is as deeply shocked and grieved as anybody else, but he is not astonished. He has never thought very highly of human nature left to itself. He has been accustomed to the idea that there is a deep interior dislocation in the very center of human personality, and that you can never, as they say, "make people good by an Act of Parliament," just because laws are man-made and therefore partake of the imperfect and self-contradictory nature of man.

Thus, in spite of the fact that humankind was created in great beauty, the current fact is, to borrow a biblical phrase, "that there is no one who is righteous," meaning to be on a par with God's original creative intentions and specifications.

Captivity or bondage—living under the stare of the snake—is a solemn experience in human life. It can be appreciated in the captivity of addictive patterns, habits, moods, and feelings about some thing or some person. We can become captive to ambitions, desires and lusts, pleasure, things, and strange appetites that elude our understanding. This is not just the homeless man on a city street who is easy to pick on. The description includes the religious leader who has fallen grievously, the investment banker who has broken the insider-trading laws in order to add to his or her private stash of millions, the white supremacist who gushes with racial hatred, and the politician who is on the take.

In these various captivities we are all unique. Each of us has a different combination and varying strengths or weaknesses concerning them. But we must bear the same label: we are sinners, captive to evil, in need of liberation that has to come from some source beyond ourselves.

The biblical writers shared a uniform perspective on the human condition that existed then and does today. Taking their cue from the ghastly Adam-Eve choice in the Garden of Eden that set a man and a woman against God's law, the poets, prophets, and apostles commented often on the severe wound that has devastated the soul. They were aware of the downward spiral of spiritual orientation and the calamitous consequences of evil that occurred in every generation. One would not be inaccurate to suggest that the biblical writers saw the soul as being cursed with a debilitating and terminal moral disease.

In my judgment, Jeremiah, the Older Testament prophet, spoke to the waterline issue of the heart more clearly than all the others. "The heart is deceitful above all things," he said, "and desperately wicked; who can know it?" (Jer. 17:9). St. Paul was uncompromising in his description: "All have sinned and fall short" (Rom. 3:23). Their mutual conclusion: it is safe to assume that we all live (or once lived) in the stare of the snake, unable to enjoy the glorious liberty of life, which was originally the gift of the Creator.

So again the question: Who has the power to break the stare of the snake? And if it is broken, what does the flight of a liberated one look like?

The biblical answer: the power lies in the sacrificial death of Jesus the Savior. What happened at the cross unleashed a power—we might call it transforming or converting power—that makes the energy of a thousand suns pale by comparison. It was an enormous event, potentially transformational for every human being.

The result? The soul—life below the waterline—can be reclaimed, returned to its original purpose: to be a dwelling place for God and a source-point for exceptional living. The evidence that this has happened? A remarkable change in spiritual orientation and a new set of attitudes, perspectives, and behaviors in life.

*Transformation* or *conversion*—old-fashioned words to some and even repugnant words to others—has to be the "starting line" word in the waterline vocabulary. It describes an experience in which a root choice is made. And that choice becomes the mother of all choices.

Robert Frost's poem on choices, "The Road Not Taken," describes the point clearly, although Frost would most likely have been horrified with the notion of connecting one of his poetic punch lines with the notion of Christian transformation. Nevertheless, he identifies a key moment in life wherein a decision maker stands at the junction of two roads and chooses. Which shall it be? The road to the right or the road to the left?

> I took the one less traveled by,
> And that has made all the difference.

There have been many dramatic examples of transformation or conversion in the history of Christianity where the stare of the snake was broken. The transformational choice of St. Augustine in a garden is dramatic. So are the choices of Martin Luther, John Newton, and John Wesley. In more recent days the transformational moment in the life of Charles Colson has been an inspiration to many.

Recently, I enjoyed a conversation with my friend Cliff Barrows—for almost fifty years the close associate of Billy Graham in all of his campaigns—in which we talked about the history of great life-change experiences. "Don't forget Jim Vaus," he said.

Instantly, I recalled the Jim Vaus story from my childhood. Vaus had been a wiretapper, an employee of the mob, a friend to virtually every gangster in the 1940s. He had heard the preaching of Billy Graham and found in the simple story of the Cross the power he sought to break the stare of the snake. His choice was dramatic with sudden results.

"I know what his conversion was like; I was there," Cliff Barrows told me. "I drove around with him in the backseat of a chauffeured limousine while we went from one person to another, from one company to another. He had long lists of all the people he had wronged or from whom he had stolen money or electronic equipment. He was determined to make restitution to every person and organization on that list. And he did it, even though it broke him financially. But when he finished, he was a totally liberated man."

My vote for one of the most powerful transformations in the history of the church is that of John Newton, writer of the hymn "Amazing Grace." To those who say that it is impossible to rebuild ruined life and character, I say, take a good look at John Newton.

Newton spent his young adult years as a slave trader, deeply involved in the transport of African people to the West Indies and to England. To read his biography is to realize that we're speaking of a man who could have hardly sunk lower in a moral sense than John Newton. If anyone has ever been caught in the stare of the snake, it was him.

But something happened, and some of it had to do with—you guessed it—a storm. On the edge of losing his life at sea in a violent hurricane, John Newton became a broken man. Suddenly, "his way" fell to pieces. And all the issues of faith came alive for him: better to know the God of the storm than to be at the mercy of the storm.

Leaving the slave trading world behind him, John Newton set out to follow Christ. The result was a final forty years of life in which Newton was one of England's finest pastors, a pastor to pastors, in fact. The debauched and totally evil man had undergone a change of life, and his character was rebuilt.

When people are transformed, what happens? There is an initial choice to abandon a previous direction in life in favor of a new direction marked out by Christ. It makes all the difference.

No conversion in history has been more of a watershed than that of St. Paul. His reorientation of life needs to be given intense study because it carries almost every detail that one might ever need to know for the purposes of experiencing a new start in life.

Almost everyone knows of Saul of Tarsus (Paul's Jewish name and place of birth) as a man of remarkable intellect and drive. A serious student of the Older Testament, a rising star in Jerusalem's religious establishment, a leader among those who resented the young, upstart Christian movement in Judaism. Saul was trained under Gamaliel, grandson to one of Israel's greatest rabbis, Hillel.

Saul's process toward transformation began with Stephen, a vibrant Christ-follower whose wisdom and capacity to handle the Scriptures were so acute that his convictions could not be refuted by the smartest of his critics. The inference of the scriptural account is that Saul or his compatriots lost badly in a debate with Stephen and were probably humiliated. If Saul had been smart, he would have quit while he was ahead. But he didn't.

Rather, he broke faith with his training and integrity and participated in a kangaroo court trial for Stephen and a resultant lynching. And when the outrageous events were ended, the scriptural camera eye zoomed in on Saul. He stood near the dying Stephen and apparently heard an incredible grace-filled prayer, "Lord, do not charge them with this sin" (Acts 7:60). In other words, forgive these folks. It was a prayer for grace on his part that Saul had not asked for or expected.

At first, Stephen's prayer seemed to have no immediate effect upon Saul. But one gets the strong impression that the words, despite Saul's resistance, found a place deep below the waterline of Saul's life—in his soul. And the words kept wafting upward like irritating smoke into Saul's nostrils, and he could not forget them.

For an indeterminate period of time after Stephen's martyrdom, Saul led an organized campaign to stamp out the swiftly spreading Christian faith. Traveling from synagogue to synagogue, town to town, Saul gridded the area (a term the air and sea rescue teams might use as they search the ocean for lost sailors) searching out followers of Christ:

> Many of the saints I shut up in prison, . . . and when they were put to death, I cast my vote against them. And I punished them often in every synagogue and compelled them to blaspheme; and being exceedingly enraged against them, I persecuted them even to foreign cities (Acts 26:10–11).

Saul's frenzied behavior is instructive. It reveals just how wild life can become when the space below the waterline of life is improperly arranged. Strangely enough, we're not looking at a man whose lifestyle is expressed in debauchery or abuse or gangsterism, to name a few unattractive alternatives. Rather, we're looking at a man whose world is religiously ordered to a fault. "Concerning the righteousness which is in the law, blameless," he could write years later as he mused upon his "pretransformational" life (Phil. 3:6), and he was not exaggerating. Religiously speaking, the man looked like a complete package.

Saul's view of reality? The view that ultimately caused him to attack Stephen and other followers of the Christ? That religion organized around the law of Moses and the temple in Jerusalem was everything. Obsession was the story of Saul's life. "Lawlikeness" was the goal. Thus, his mission was to seek out Gentiles who were sympathetic to Judaism and convince them to undergo all the appropriate rites, which would mean that they'd renounced their gentile identity and embraced Judaism. If anyone could have done that, Saul was the man.

When Paul later wrote that he "compelled [Christians] to blaspheme," he was clearly referring to an inquisitorial event that took place in synagogues when Jews were given something akin to a heresy trial. Those were often accompanied—especially in the case of men—with a humiliating and life-threatening beating of thirty-nine lashes with a leather metal-tipped whip. Many did not survive the beating physically or psychically.

During this "trial," the defendant was given the right to make a defense, and the plaintiffs were obligated to listen. Why is this important? Because it suggests that Saul must have been forced to listen to countless "witnesses" to Christ-following faith. And he must have heard similar themes over and over again that amounted to one thing: transformation, life change, new direction, a different set of choices. And all of it must have been reminiscent of Stephen as he watched others suffer and even die with the same grace and determination. Suddenly, all of Saul's hard-earned brilliance and dedication was worthless in the face of a genre of people whose life below the waterline could not be impeached.

It was in this obsessive pattern that Saul found himself on the way to Damascus, fourteen days journey northeast of Jerusalem, to continue his savage attacks on the rapidly dispersing and growing Christian community:

At midday . . . along the road I saw a light from heaven, brighter than the sun, shining around me and those who journeyed with me. . . . I heard a voice speaking to me. . . . "Saul, Saul, why are you persecuting Me? It is hard for you to kick against the goads" (Acts 26:13–14).

It wasn't long before Saul of Tarsus, knocked off his animal into the dust, was aware that he was in the presence of Jesus.

One account says that Saul launched with two questions: "Who are You, Lord?" and "What do You want me to do?" (Acts 9:5–6). These, it seems to me, are the classic questions around which all transformations revolve.

From Stephen to a mass of witnesses to Jesus of Nazareth clothed in a bright light—a light so bright that it darkened the midday desert sun—Saul was forced into a succession of disruptive moments—John Newton's storm, Augustine's crisis in the garden. And the conversion process commenced the minute he addressed the figure in the heavenly vision as Lord and further signified his submission with the question, "What do You want me to do?"

Was Saul's transformation complete in the wake of those two questions? I don't think so. The Damascus road event could have gone down as little more than a spiritual experience, a spectacular moment that might have burned out like a shooting star, if it had not been followed by an almost immediate deepening awareness of what Christ was asking. And that came through subsequent encounters with mentors and spiritual directors in following days, the most notable of whom was Ananias. Paul had a long way to go before transformation could be said to have fully taken place.

When Saul had his confrontational experience on the road to Damascus, he was blinded into helplessness. For several days he was completely dependent upon those who would lead him about. Not until Ananias, a Christ-follower living in Damascus, came and addressed him as "brother" (a remarkable thing in itself), placed his hands upon him, and prayed for him was Saul's sight restored. One assumes that Paul never forgot the terrible experience of blindness, which symbolized his spiritual helplessness.

All of the trauma was a disruptive moment. Was it crisis? Wonderment? Both? It was an experience over which a man used to controlling all things had no control. And it was an experience he could hardly, if at all, explain. Disruption to be sure! He had been traveling to Damascus with all the confidence of a powerful leader; he had arrived humbled in blindness and inner stupefaction. The very One whose name he'd come to stamp out had ambushed him on the road and sent him on his way a fledgling follower. The snake's stare had been broken again.

Saul emerged from a party of people—the Pharisees—who had enjoyed several hundred years of religious success and domination. But when Jesus came and offered them a new way of seeing things, they were unable to see the possibilities of spiritual breakthrough. And Saul was a foremost example of their stubbornness. So resistant had he become that persecution became his game.

That is why the Damacus road experience is so poignant. Its dramatic confrontation was so powerful that Saul's old view of reality was shattered, broken into pieces. And what reformed within his soul was a new view of reality. Lawlikeness—the old version— became Christlikeness—a new version. And Saul never got over the disruptive moment, which led to personal transformation.

Building the necessary weight below the waterline of life begins here. It demands an authentic experience of inner transformation.

Here I want to enter a second word into the waterline vocabulary. Not a new word but a familiar one used differently. For I see Saul of Tarsus now not only converted but *converting*.

Years later Saul (now Paul) would write to the Corinthians about transformation: "We . . . are being transformed into the same image from glory to glory, just as by the Spirit of the Lord" (2 Cor. 3:18).

*Converted* and *converting*. Key words as one moves beneath the waterline and seeks the meaning and significance of change.

Saul was of course never the same. Over the next ten years, he passed through a process often marked with pain and struggle that reshaped his soul. Every event—many painful beyond description—added powerful new weight below the waterline until he was a virtually unshakable human being. The raw energy, which had—in earlier years—driven him to steep himself in Older Testament Scriptures and seek leadership in the temple community of Jerusalem, became a refined energy, which sent him forth about the Roman world to preach the gospel; plant churches, and polish young leaders into a formidable movement that exists until this day.

The people of my faith tradition put great emphasis upon transformation or conversion. When they gathered for church, they made an effort to call folks to conversion at the end of virtually every service of worship. Their attention was so riveted upon this one moment of conversion that they often misunderstood the significance of the lifelong process that followed: that of converting.

Saul (who became Paul as he journeyed in the gentile world) saw himself in a continued state of converting or transforming. Even as an old man when his body was giving up on him, he was quick to write: "Our inner man is being renewed day by day" (2 Cor. 4:16 NASB).

The stare of the snake was broken that day on the road to Damascus when Jesus came shouting and waving His arms. But

Paul was always aware that the snake wished to return, to assert the old hegemony if he could. So for the old Apostle every day was another challenge to build below the waterline, to complete the process of transformation. And it worked.

# WHAT KIND OF AN OLD MAN DO YOU WANT TO BE?

*Tho' much is taken, much abides: and tho'*
*We are not now that strength which in old days*
*Moved earth and heaven; that which we are, we are;*
*One equal temper of heroic hearts,*
*Made weak by time and fate, but strong in will*
*To strive, to seek, to find, and not to yield.*
*—Tennyson, "Ulysses"*

THERE IS A brief but charming story hidden in the Older Testament. Its major player is an old man, Caleb, who makes infrequent appearances in a forty-year-plus slice of the history of the Hebrew people.

Caleb's first appearance of significance came when he was one of twelve men entrusted by Moses with the responsibility of exploring Canaan in anticipation of a Hebrew invasion. He and Joshua—Moses' successor—seem to have become closely connected. That much was apparent when the twelve returned from the mission. The reconnaissance report was in two parts: a majority report from ten of the men and a minority report from Joshua and Caleb.

The report of the ten was gloomy. The good news, the ten said, was that the land was abundant with wealth and resources, the kind of place anyone would like as a home. But the bad news was that there were giants in the land who'd gotten there first. By comparison, the ten spies compared themselves to grasshoppers.

Joshua and Caleb saw it differently. Yes, they admitted, there were people who seemed like giants, but the God of Israel had faced down "giants" before, and that was no time to think it would be any different. As far as the two-man minority was concerned, there was no time like the present to move ahead and draw on the promises and power of God.

But Israel sided with the majority, and as a consequence, the people spent the next forty years hiking about in wild country as an entire generation of faithless people died off. All, of course, except Joshua and Caleb.

In terms of Scripture Caleb is not heard from during much of the forty years. But apparently, the man never changed from the feisty, faith-driven fellow who'd once been ready to lead the charge into the land of the giants. Now, four decades later, another generation of Hebrews—under Joshua's direction—massed at the Jordan River, not far from Jericho, and plotted another invasion. When they crossed over the river, they were successful in almost every one of their endeavors, and before long, a massive percentage of Canaan was theirs to control. Except the hill country.

The hill country was where the Anakites were said to live. The Anakites, a legendary tribe of people reported as formidable in height and fighting ability. Both the people and the terrain were enough to intimidate all but the bravest, and no one stepped forward to take on the challenge.

No one except Caleb! In his mid-eighties! The biblical account of his conversation with Joshua—much worth reading—goes like this:

[Caleb said to Joshua], "You know what the LORD said to Moses the man of God at Kadèsh Barnea about you and me. I was forty years old when Moses . . . sent me from Kadesh Barnea to explore the land. And I brought him back a report according to my convictions, but my brothers who went up with me made the hearts of the people melt with fear. I, however, followed the LORD my God wholeheartedly. So on that day Moses swore to me, 'The land on which your feet have walked will be your inheritance and that of your children forever, because you have followed the LORD my God wholeheartedly.'

"Now then, just as the LORD promised, he has kept me alive for forty-five years since the time he said this to Moses, while Israel moved about in the desert. So here I am today, eighty-five years old! I am still as strong today as the day Moses sent me out; I'm just as vigorous to go out to battle now as I was then. Now give me this hill country that the LORD promised me that day. You yourself heard then that the Anakites were there and their cities were large and fortified, but, the LORD helping me, I will drive them out just as he said."

Then Joshua blessed Caleb . . . and gave him Hebron as his inheritance. So Hebron has belonged to Caleb . . . ever since, because he followed the LORD, the God of Israel, wholeheartedly (Josh. 14:6–14 NIV).

Three times the word *wholeheartedly* is used to describe a man who spent his life living out of the soul. One gains a sense that Caleb organized his life about the promises of God. The result is seen in the kind of old man he became. His toughness, his enthusiasm, and his enormous faith are no accident. They flow from below his personal waterline.

Today, men and women in their eighty-fifth year are not uncommon. But old men like Caleb are! His vitality shouts loud. This brief story reveals a man with these qualities:

• Whatever he has done, he has done wholeheartedly, nothing held back.

• He was always a man who had strong convictions and lived by them.

• He is a man who continues to love challenges and prefers the toughest of them all.

• He is a man who has unlimited faith that the God of his youth is the God of his old age.

• If others are fearful, he isn't; if you'll stand back, he'll swing into motion.

Tell me, how many men or women do you know like that? I ask this question because it becomes a highly significant one when we begin to explore what it means to live out of the soul, to pay attention to issues below the waterline. If we are to live out of the soul, we must walk in the company of those who have done so before us and offer the experiences of a "cloud of witnesses."

When I crossed the line into my fifties, I found myself in one of those disruptive moments described in an earlier chapter. The moment came under the heading of the aging process, and I began to tussle with a new question: *What kind of an old man do you want to be?* It was a waterline question.

Lately, I've been talking about this question with frequency. Sometimes people smile when I present this question. They think I'm fooling with an idea. I'm not.

The question—What kind of an old man do you want to be?— was not designed to describe where I wanted to live in my older years (I like New England). And it was not centered on the matter of finances (which I hope will be adequate). Rather, the question had to do with character, personality, and a style of being.

Frankly, what drove the question in part was a sober observation: the senior years are not commonly considered to be the most attractive ones for most people. If my observations are correct, I shouldn't expect to be invited out to a lot of ball games by younger people when I'm old.

That unpleasant possibility bothered me. Because I realized that, barring a premature life-ending event, I would be joining the ranks of the old in the not-too-distant future and younger men would be saying the same thing about men of my generation. I just might be included in their comments.

But Caleb seems to be the kind of man who would make the small list of exceptions. You get the feeling you'd not only like to take him to a ball game, but you'd like to follow him around whenever possible and enjoy the strength of his character and determination.

Caleb is not alone when one looks back to the old men of the Bible. There are some wonderful people there. Enoch, it is said, "walked with God" (Gen. 5:22). Of Abraham, it was written, he "died in a good old age . . . full of years" (Gen. 25:8). Something positive about an old man there. Moses left life with this epitaph: "No one has ever shown the mighty power or performed the awesome deeds that Moses did" (Deut. 34:12 NIV).

Other men of the Bible wielded powerful and positive influence in their older years. Take Joshua, for example: "Israel served the LORD all the days of Joshua" (Josh. 24:31). Still others were marked with a quality of faithfulness in spirit that was rewarded by God. Simeon who prophesied over Jesus the baby in the temple "was just and devout, waiting for the Consolation of Israel, and the Holy Spirit was upon him" (Luke 2:25). And Paul in self-assessment said, "I am already being poured out. . . . I have fought the good fight . . . I have kept the faith" (2 Tim. 4:6–7).

As I said, one gets the feeling that they would have been good men to know. And one also has the perception that their last years were among their very best.

And that was the very first thing I decided might be important as I confronted the question, *What kind of an old man do you want to be?* My answer: a man who is pleasant to be around because he is doing his best work and shows his highest character in his last years.

With that in mind, I started compiling a register of old men I knew who were—by my estimate—at their peak in life in their last years. One thing quickly became clear. I have known a lot of old men, but my list of "emulatable" old men was alarmingly short.

In the making of my list, I had deleted many possible names for a host of reasons. Some who could have made the list didn't because they had permitted themselves to drift into self-centeredness and took minimal interest in the lives and thoughts of others. Others didn't make my list because they were impatient with youth and saw little, if anything, good about the ideas and achievements of the young.

There were still other reasons my list was brief. A quality of crustiness, meanness, or irritability about the edges of the aging personality might hint that this unfortunate quality had always been there but had been covered up most of the time in the past. As I watched carefully, I saw some who seemed bent on a later life of complaining criticism.

I noted that many simply lived in the past and saw little interest in laying down the red carpet for the upcoming generations as they moved toward the future. In short, I found a host of reasons for cutting old men from the list of those whom one might want to be like.

As I said, when the list was finished, it included just a few names. In fact, I could count the names on the fingers of one hand. The list would have been larger of course if I'd included women, but being a man, I decided to stick with my own gender, and each one I selected was in his seventies, eighties, or nineties.

Each man on the list is different in personality, and I even have the suspicion that if some of them met, they might not be drawn to one another. But as I pondered the men and who they are, I kept asking, What are the qualities that can only be ascribed to a wholehearted (Caleb-like) lifestyle, one that lives out of the soul?

The word *gratitude* was the first thing that came to mind. All of them are appreciative. Their conversation, their correspondence, and their responses to events are all marked with appreciation. They are quick to recognize what anyone does for them or for others. And they are swift to let people know when they have acted for the benefit of others.

The quality of gratitude is at the center of a healthy soul. St. Paul took note of it when he wrote in the Roman letter that the first mark of a decadent culture was its thanklessness (Rom. 1:21). Whether talking of cultures or friendships, one of the first things to go when vitality is lost is the theme of gratitude.

And gratitude appears to take a licking in the aging process. It is replaced by a sense of entitlement, of grudging demands. In contrast, the spirit of thankfulness does not come naturally. It must be worked at as a discipline for most of us.

Many years ago one of the old men on my list came to visit in our home for several days. Because of his international reputation as a Christian leader, he had every right to demand a hotel accommodation, but he was pleased to stay as a guest in our home. Because our home was of modest size, we asked our son to give up his bedroom for our guest.

It wasn't many days after our guest had departed that the mail carrier brought a letter to our son, Mark. It was from our friend, and it expressed strong gratitude for his gracious relinquishing of his room for an older man. Our son kept that letter on his bulletin board for many years. I came to learn that this sort of expression of appreciation for the smallest thing was a characteristic of this man's life.

Gratitude demands a keen eye to notice the things easily overlooked. But the old men of whom I speak have the eye, and they never stop saying thank you: to God for good health and new opportunities, to their spouses for their love, to their friends for their encouragement and companionship, to the younger people who come to them and draw from their strength.

A second mark of the old men that made my list is *their enthusiastic interest in the accomplishments of the younger generation*. They take great delight in what they see younger comrades able to accomplish. They are the first to lead the cheers, the first to express approval in new achievements.

And the younger misunderstand if they think this is easy. For there is an almost irresistible temptation to drift into jealousy or to minimize what one sees another of a younger generation able to do. The thought comes almost involuntarily, *Why couldn't I have done that?* as the older is reminded once again that leadership and initiative are passing on to a new generation.

The old men on my list have come to peace with this reality. They not only have no resentment for those who are younger; they have committed themselves to making the younger successful whenever possible.

When I study the commonalities of the men on my list, *I'm impressed with the fact that they have all chosen to keep their minds sharp and agile*. Unlike so many others, they have not stopped thinking, not ceased grasping for new ideas. They are like Caleb, who yearns to tackle the hill country. They revel in things new.

So my men read, and they read broadly and deeply. They are into theology, current events, history, the emerging technologies, the cultural paradigm shifts of our time. They are conversant with the language, and they have their own convictions about where and how things are going. Though not brittle, they have their opinions, and they know how to express them when asked. Theirs is a world-view not of yesterday but of today. Change is not their enemy but their friend.

One is as likely to hear that one of these men has just finished reading a Shakespeare play as he is to hear of a new book reviewed in the Sunday *New York Times*. And one may hear of a concern for a piece of public policy or the trading of a first-round draft choice for an old veteran in the NFL.

One character trait that has influenced me concerning my older friends is *their ability to think in what I like to call macro-terms*. They are big-picture people. They look at life from the largest point of view, and they resist panic when sudden events grab the headlines and younger people are sure that the end of time has arrived.

Macro-thinking takes into account the long flow of history and how God works in slow, almost imperceptible ways. And here is the paradox. While my favorite men know how to change, they resist change for change's sake. Or to say it this way, they sense the difference between fad and substantial change. They are unimpressed with the former; they know how to bend with the latter.

Caleb was a macro-thinker. He'd seen God work over and over again, and "he followed him wholeheartedly." The hill country and the Anakites might cripple the spirit of some who had little history with the God of Israel, but not Caleb. He had enough experience encoded in his soul that taking the hill country seemed only something of mild exertion.

*The kind of old man I want to be never retires.* He'd become bored instantly. Walk away from a job? Sure. But retire, never. That's because these kinds of old men settled the issue of what they want to do when they grow up a long time ago. It was described in something like a life-mission or sense of call.

In the case of my favorite old men, the mission begins with the notion of giving and not taking. They are called to the notion that life and vitality are in the act of adding value to the generations.

One friend whom I highly value came to visit me one day, and we began to talk about the coming days when we would lay aside our jobs and go on to other things.

"There are two things that I think I'd like to do when more of my time is my own," my friend said. "First, I'd like to buy a van and fill it full of tools. Then I'd drive the community in search of elderly people who need a handyman to fix things. Too often they're taken advantage of by contractors who charge them an arm and a leg for simple repairs. I can see myself doing that sort of thing and then being able to talk with them about the faith I have that makes me want to do things like that.

"The other thing sounds sort of crazy, but every time I hike some of the paths through the woods around where I live, I think of how much I'd like to give time to maintaining those paths someday. It would give me a lot of satisfaction to know that others were having a great time enjoying creation because I made their walkway a bit nicer."

Here is a man who has no intention of retiring. His focus of work is simply changing from that of income production to value production. And these two wishes characterize the kind of life he's lived all of his adulthood and will continue to live in the last third of his life.

I saw this emerging perspective in him almost twenty years ago when we were much younger. I was the pastor of a growing congregation, and he was a member of the highest leadership board. He would sit at the side of the chairman of the board and write the minutes of the meetings. No one who has ever seen those minutes will ever fail to distinguish them from all other minutes of meetings he or she has ever seen. The handwriting was in an unusual printed format, easy to read. There was a clear record of all significant things said at the meeting, and there were occasional nuggets of humor that made the record a pleasure to read.

One weekend this group of church leaders went away on a retreat. We found ourselves sitting about a fireplace on the first evening, and I tried to set the mood by opening a bit of the personal side of my life and dreams in hope that it would spark conversation from others at a more intimate level. My effort was successful, and soon other men were taking turns telling their stories and something of what was important to them.

It came time for my friend to speak. As best as I can recall his words—and they so impressed me that I have never forgotten them—he said, "I guess I am what you call a servant. I enjoy making other people look good. In my job I often report to people several levels above me who know that I'll give them my best to get their projects done and not take any of their glory away. They need it, and I really don't. So it makes them more willing to trust me."

I was astonished by my friend's words. He was a highly educated, brilliant engineer. In fact, he has been a "major player" (as they like to say) in one of the most highly classified and significant military projects of the past decade. But more important than his technical expertise and his need to expand a career was his sense of what servanthood meant. And now twenty years later as he prepares to step away from his job, the fact is that he is not retiring. He will merely transfer his role of servanthood to another theater of operation.

Oh, yes. One more story about my friend. Just a few weeks ago (from the first writing of this chapter), our church produced its annual Christmas production, a musical with Christmas themes that attracts many thousands of people. For more than a dozen years my friend has been a part of the stage crew moving scenery and props. Now we are talking about a man in his sixties, who rides his bicycle to his office almost every day, who chooses to work behind the scenes in a younger man's task.

I went behind the stage one night while the musical was in progress, and there he was with a couple of the younger men. They were all dressed in the appropriate stagehand black from head to toe, waiting to make the next stage change.

"Have you seen the show out in front?" I asked. "It's absolutely fantastic," I added.

"No," my friend said. "We never really get to see all of it. Working back here is like sitting on the back side of your television set, hearing the sounds, and trying to imagine what others are seeing on the screen." It was all said in humor. But the truth was there. If some are going to see the show, others will have to be backstage. And that is the way my friend has lived, and that pretty much describes the sort of old man he'll be.

The old man I want to be owns a characteristic I see in short supply today. But I see it in the men on my list. It's a quality I can only identify with these words: *tenderness and compassion*. I can describe what I'm driving at better than I can give it a word or two.

In a discussion with a group of men, I asked, "Who has been the most influential man in your personal life?" Of the dozen or more who had joined the conversation, the majority identified their grandfathers as the most influential. Their observation was for me a surprise, but it shouldn't have been. Soon we were immersed in grandfather stories, and in almost every case the themes were the same.

Grandfather was the laid-back, slow-to-react, tender sort of man who almost connived with you against your parents. Fathers and mothers were preoccupied with their own growing up, doing things exactly right, making sure nothing went wrong for the moment. But grandfathers (and grandmothers)? Another story!

"Let me tell you a story that characterizes the kind of man my grandfather was," one man said to us. "He was a farmer, and he had all the regular kinds of farm machinery—trucks, tractors, that sort of thing—and he taught me how to drive each of them in the summer. Well, there was this one day—I was about twelve—when he and I were out in a field, and he said to me, 'Run back to the barn and bring the truck out here.' I was thrilled that he'd asked, and I went to the barn, got into the truck, and started to back it out. But I turned the wheels too quickly, and suddenly, I had the front bumper of the truck wedged into the side of the door. And it seemed if I went forward or backward, I was going to hurt either the truck or the barn. I was devastated because I figured that Granddad would see that I wasn't old enough to be driving his machinery.

"But I had no choice in the matter, so I went back out to the field and said, 'Granddad, you've got to come and help me. The truck's stuck in the doorway.' He stood there for a moment quietly looking at me, stroking his short beard. And then he said, 'Son, it seems to me that you got the thing stuck; you can go back and get it unstuck.' I never loved my grandfather more than I did at that moment."

After we'd all laughed, he continued, "Now, my father would have said something like, 'Can't I ever trust you to do a thing right? How many times do I have to tell you how to do something? Come on, I'll do it myself!' Not my grandfather. He knew something about how important it was for a boy to keep his dignity even if it meant a little crinkle in the fender of a farm truck."

The story well celebrates what I have in mind. Kindness, patience, grace. Being a gracious person who understands the larger issues in life, that there are things more important than perfection, deadlines, and accumulation. There is rather the enlarging of the person. And that is what noble old men do best.

My old men have another quality about them: *they still love their wives dearly, even romantically.* I'm talking about some old men I know who delight in their marriages after forty or fifty years. Who reach out to touch their wives with tender affection, who maintain a twinkle in their eyes when they look in their wives' direction, who speak in endearing terms whenever they converse.

But more than those traits, I speak of men who have never stopped caring for the wife's growth, for her care and comfort, for her quality of life. My old men share a rigorous spiritual journey with their wives; they talk over important decisions; they know how to have fun together. When they speak of their wives, they speak in noble tones, and each man does nothing but heap praise and appreciation upon the one with whom he's walked through the majority of life.

That just didn't happen. It was a habit of relationship from the very first. And it makes the latter years the softest and the best.

Gail and I sit with one of our favorite older couples. We notice how his hand often reaches out to pat hers when they speak. We're impressed with how they look each other in the eye, how they compliment each other about appearance, how even humorous exchanges are couched in the deepest respect.

"Do you ever have conflicts after sixty years of marriage?" Gail asks.

"Of course we do," comes the answer. "Why, just this morning E——[the wife] was driving, and she didn't make a full stop at a stop sign. And so I said, 'E——, later on when there's a better time, I have a thought for you.'"

He went on, "Now you see, I learned a long time ago that E——is very sensitive about criticism. She had a father who could be very mean, and he often badly hurt her feelings when she was a child. So I'm careful not to say things that will remind her of those moments, and the best thing to do is to wait until she can handle my criticism."

I was incredulous: "Are you telling me that there are still sensitivities that can be hurt that go back eighty years?"

"Absolutely," my old-man-hero responded. "Some of these things are never forgotten, and if you're going to love each other in your old age, they can never be overlooked. You've got to be just as careful not to hurt each other in your old age as you were in your youth. So tonight, after we've had a good meal and we're sitting on the porch watching the sun go down, and we're very happy with each other, I'll say, 'E——, I love you very much, but this morning when we were driving, you really blew it.'"

We spend an enormous amount of energy during most of our lives working with the issues of power and control. Obviously, each of us has to have a little of both. But perhaps one of the most painful aspects of the aging process for many men and women is the reality that power and control are likely to be lost.

For some old people, this is the reason for creeping bitterness and a reactionary personality. They cannot stand the loss of the power they once had. Power over their bodies, their relationships, their work, and their organizations (including the church).

But there are different kinds of power. *Wise old men do not try to hold on to institutional power.* They do not try to control people. They take care of their bodies, of course, but they are not surprised—and life doesn't end for them—when even their health fails a bit.

Because the old men I revere have lived out of the soul, they become increasingly aware of another kind of power: the power of intercession with God and the power of wisdom. *These old men know how to pray, and they have come to realize that there are no more vital moments than those in which they are in close contact with God.*

As I noted before, Simeon, the old man in the temple at the

time of Christ's birth, was this kind of man. Of him, it was said, "There was a man in Jerusalem whose name was Simeon, and this man was just and devout, waiting for the Consolation of Israel, and the Holy Spirit was upon him" (Luke 2:25).

We don't know much about Simeon, except that when Mary and Joseph brought the newborn Jesus to the temple, Simeon was able to discern immediately the uniqueness of this baby in contrast to all others who were brought to the temple every day.

I have often wondered what that encounter must have been like when Simeon took Jesus into his arms and blessed Him, the old man and the newborn infant. Simeon seems to have been the first person—apart from Mary herself—to realize the full implications of this child. From the depths of his soul he discerned truths about this baby that no one else could perceive. He foresaw and affirmed Jesus' mission and the reactions of the people.

> This Child is destined for the fall and rising of many in Israel, and for a sign which will be spoken against [this was a word to Mary] (yes, a sword will pierce through your own soul also), that the thoughts of many hearts may be revealed (Luke 2:34–35).

Only Simeon saw all of this: how Jesus would turn things upside down, how many would take extreme offense at His ministry, how many would be driven to repentance and others to resistance, how Mary's heart would be broken, most likely through the events of the Cross. It took an old man—filled at soul-level with the Spirit of God—to see and identify what the rest of the world in its power pursuits was too preoccupied to see and respond to.

My old men remind me of Simeon. They have stepped aside to let younger men and women run programs and organizations. They do not have to be the speaker on every occasion. In fact, they are quiet enough that others plead with them to speak. They no longer compete; they don't have to. And when they must communicate, they appreciate the importance of having first spoken with heaven before they speak with people in real time.

An old man I greatly admire died a few years ago. We were having breakfast together a year or two before his death. He was in his early eighties. As we ate, he was telling me of a recent errand he'd pursued that made it necessary for him to drive into Boston.

"On the way down the turnpike, I stopped at a rest stop for a time of prayer," he said.

"What did you have to pray about?" I asked.

"Well, I was driving along and realized that I was going to have to walk through the Combat Zone [Boston's then infamous red-light district]. I knew that I'd have to pass some of those pornographic magazine stores and massage parlors, and I'd need the Lord's help to avoid the temptation to look in."

"Now, wait a minute, L——," I said, a bit bluntly. "I don't want to offend you, but you're a man in his eighties. Are you telling me that you are still facing sexual temptations in your thought life and that you have to pray in order to control them? I thought that when I was—"

"Young man," my friend interrupted me, "just because I'm eighty-two doesn't mean the red blood has stopped running. And if you don't learn how to pray more fervently, these things will bother you, too, when you're old."

The old men I want to be like have reached a point in life when they fully understand the biblical words, "Without Me you can do nothing." And they have no need to fight this truth. They watch younger men and women straining hard to build power bases, control people, structures, and money, speak out of such smartness, and they smile. Because they've learned that "this is *not* where it's at." So they gladly relinquish these things to the younger while they relax in the value of quiet, unbroken intersect with God.

There is one final thing I'd like to say about the old men on my short list of men I'd like to be like: *they are not afraid of death.* Dying bothers them as it does me. Some of us have laughed when we've talked about these things. There are a hundred ways to die, we tell one another. Only two of them are attractive ways. The other ninety-eight are to be avoided.

But death? Fear? Never! These men fully understand St. Paul's admitted conflict when he spoke of his impending death:

> For to me, to live is Christ, and to die is gain. But if I live on in the flesh, this will mean fruit from my labor; yet what I shall choose I cannot tell. For I am hard pressed between the two, having a desire to depart and be with Christ, which is far better. Nevertheless to remain in the flesh is more needful for you (Phil. 1:21–24).

They are not living in a fantasy, these old-men friends of mine. They enjoy life, and they are happy to go on indefinitely. As long as they can serve, contribute value, build the younger, shine as lights for the glory of God.

Such a man was Caleb. We don't know a lot about this man's outer life—how tall he was, how successful he was at making a living, how large a family he had, whether or not he had a memorable sense of humor. If he'd been a modern man, we'd be saying, we don't know where he went to college, what company he worked for, or how high he got on the corporate ladder. We don't know how far he traveled, how much money he made, or how athletic he was.

But we do know something about Caleb's soul. That what he did, he did wholeheartedly—from the soul. And that when he was eighty-five, he was ready to take on the Anakites in the hills. I don't know much about this man, but I'm going to tell you this one thing in conclusion: I'd like to be like him when I grow up.

# A SOUL SHAPED BY MISSION

*No one knows where he is going; the
aim of life has been forgotten and the
end has been left behind. Man has set
out at a tremendous pace—to go
nowhere.*
*—Jacques Ellul*

A MAN IN our congregation was president of a Boston-based insurance company. We often visited in his office for breakfast or lunch. I found the conversations stimulating as they swept back and forth between personal issues, the church of which we were both part, and the nature of his business life.

One day the subject was business. Knowing his company to be very diverse in its interests and activities, I asked him if it were possible to boil the organization's activities down to the simplest possible description. He said, "That's easy. You're asking what our mission is, and we know what it is . . . all of us. The mission of our company is. . . ."

The completion of his sentence was a concise statement about thirty words long. It was spoken with such smoothness and clarity that I knew I was hearing something that had been carefully crafted, memorized, quoted often, and now embraced as a strong conviction. When he finished, he added, "And my job as chief executive officer is to assure our board of directors that the mission gets carried·out to the fullest possible extent." I believed him. You could see the determination in his eyes.

Some hours after that conversation, I visited with another exec-utive in the same organization who was also a friend. Somewhere in our conversation, I mentioned the aims and objective of the company and was startled when he nodded and repeated the same statement I'd heard earlier. And he did it exactly as I'd heard it earlier, word for word.

But I remained unappreciative of the significance of what I was hearing until I had one more conversation, this time with a third member of the same business. With more amusement in mind than anything else, I said, "Hey, I'm just curious. If someone were to ask you about the business of this company, what would you . . . ?"

"I'd start with our mission statement," came the reply. "It goes like this: the mission of—"

"I've heard it," I said, interrupting him. "It sounds almost as if everyone, even the boys in the mailroom, may have memorized it like a Bible verse."

"Yeah, we all have," he replied. "Mailroom's down the hall. Go down there and see if I'm right."

I was neither a rocket scientist nor an MBA from Harvard Business School, but I knew I'd learned something about organiza-tional leadership I'd never fully appreciated before. This: that a large company employing scores of people must find a way to describe in the most simple terms *why* it opens its doors each day, *what* is supposed to happen, and *how* each person can maximize his or her contribution to the overall effort.

To the extent that people do not understand the company's "business" or mission, there will be confusion of effort, breakdown in communication and, certainly, a trend toward disaster. When I left those offices and drove out of Boston toward Lexington that day many years ago, I reflected on what I'd learned: that organizations (and this includes marriages, families, churches, governments) are no stronger than the shared sense of mission that is described and written in the hearts and minds of the people who are a part of them.

That visit and its learning experience happened long before a plethora of management books began to emerge telling business leaders the same thing. Then came Stephen Covey with his brilliant book *The 7 Habits of Highly Effective People* taking the principle a step further. He proposed that people need a definition of personal mission every bit as much as companies do.

Go back for a moment to the day Michael Plant left New York on his ill-fated voyage. Imagine him saying to those asking where he was headed, "I'm not sure. It's a wonderful month for sailing, the ocean offers lots of options, so I'm just going to go where the wind and currents take me."

In Plant's case, the mission was obvious. Get to France.

If one's mission is too small, too vague, too parochial, there is the supreme danger of ending up being driven by someone else's mission.

> I read how Quixote in his random ride,
> Came to a crossing once,
>     and lest he lose
> The purity of chance, would not decide
> Wither to fare, but wished his
>     horse to choose.
> For glory lay where ever he might turn.
> His head was light with pride,
>     his horse's shoes
> Were heavy, and he headed
>     for the barn. (Richard Wilbur)

Why is all of this important? Easy: this book is about the inner person, that strange territory sometimes referred to as the soul. And souls tend to drift. They shouldn't; they weren't created to; but they do. Souls were meant to be in intimate touch with the Creator, but they're not. The tragic severance happened the day—as the Bible tells the story—that the first generation made wrong choices and became captive to sin. Something of great significance in the soul fell into great despair: its ability to provide guidance to the rest of the person.

In the book *Mr. Bridge* novelist Evan Connell describes a moment in the life of a Kansas City lawyer of the 1930s. Outwardly, he is seen in the community as the epitome of success. He is wealthy; his family seems strong; he is highly respected. But that's life—as we say—above the waterline. At soul-level—below the waterline—Mr. Bridge is a bundle of hidden fears.

Awake in the middle of the night and staring out of the window as a storm rages, Bridge ponders the direction of his life:

> A leaf flattened itself against the window beside his head and leaped away in the darkness, and a feeling of profound despair came over him because everything he had done was useless. All that he believed in and had attempted to prove seemed meager, all of his life was wasted.

Mr. Bridge's nocturnal thoughts are not unique. Poet Ed Sissman had similar ideas when he wrote,

> Men past forty,
> Get up nights,
> Look out at city lights
> And wonder
> Where they made the wrong turn
> And why life is so long.

Thoughts of this genre remind us that a sense of direction is a highly significant matter for the soul. The soul has to be given direction. And one could say the direction has to be reaffirmed with frequency lest it be forgotten. In part that is done by the development of a sense of mission.

Thus, a *mission*, as we are using the word, is a foundational intention that provides meaning and direction to all of life. A mission well-defined will provide the grounds for guidance, choice making, and values throughout one's life.

In his landmark book *The Fifth Discipline*, Peter Senge quotes Bill O'Brien, CEO of Hanover Insurance,

> People enter business as bright, well-educated, high energy people, full of energy and desire to make a difference. By the time they are 30, a few are on the fast track and the rest put in their time and do what matters to them on the weekend. They lose the commitment, the sense of mission, and the excitement with which they started their careers. We get . . . little of their energy and almost none of their spirit.

Then Senge goes on,

> Surprisingly few adults work to rigorously develop their own personal mastery. When you ask most adults what they want from their lives, they often talk first about what they'd like to get rid of. . . . *The discipline of personal mastery, by contrast, starts with clarifying the things that really matter to us, of living our lives in the service of our highest aspirations*. (emphasis mine)

One of the things that draws us to the men and women of the Bible is that they show us this evidence of personal mastery. They show it, first of all, when we see them living in a mission-driven mode.

Take the Older Testament prophet Ezra for an example. His mission: "For Ezra had prepared his heart to seek the Law of the LORD, and to do it, and to teach statutes and ordinances in Israel"

(Ezra 7:10). Possibly, that was a standard statement for men like Ezra in his time. Nevertheless, the three-point mission—study, obey, and teach—was the sum total of Ezra's life. Everything was guided by those three supreme pursuits in his life.

Moses' sense of mission began to emerge in the first third of his life. In its most basic form it became the liberation of his people, the Hebrews. His first attempt at pursuing his mission was poorly timed and carried out. On impulse he killed an Egyptian overseer, apparently thinking it would alert the Hebrew people and initiate something of a movement. It didn't. And soon Moses was fleeing for his life.

Forty years later, the mission was reaffirmed. But this time on God's terms and in God's way. The mission was still the liberation of the Hebrews, but the tactics were a bit different. If there must be violence, God will handle it. Moses was faithful to the mission as it was carried out: get the people out of Egypt, teach them the law of God, and guide them to the Promised Land.

St. Paul had a mission. You can see it referred to in various forms, but the most succinct statement of it is in his Colossian letter: "[Christ] we preach, warning every [person] and teaching every [person] in all wisdom, that we may present every [person] perfect in Christ[likeness]" (Col. 1:28).

"What business are you in, Paul?" I hear someone ask him.

"I'm in the people-development business," I hear him answer.

"What would your developed people look like?" comes the follow-up question.

"They'd have the characteristics of Jesus," the response.

"So how do you develop these people if that's your mission?"

"I tell them about Christ; I convince them to follow Him as Lord and Savior. Then I spend lots of time with them working together (tent making, you know). We do lots of talking together, and I try to show them Jesus not only in words but in my life. And then I get them to join with other followers and make congregations. Everyone grows that way."

Jesus Christ had a mission. And He never deviated from it. Even when His closest friends and His most vigorous critics tried to dissuade Him.

Jericho, city of. Luke describes a day when Jesus passes through on His way to Jerusalem. He is within a few days of His crucifixion. But no one knows that. All His friends assume is that they will be in Jerusalem for the Passover days and that there just could be something of an uprising or a revival or a stupendous demonstration of great proportion. There is no room for thinking crucifixion in the minds of the friends of Jesus.

As they are walking, a cry comes from the side of the road: "Jesus, Son of David, have mercy on me!" (Luke 18:38).

Those closest to the one who has shouted tell him to shut up. He's poor, worthless, and blind. Jesus Christ will not have time to stop for him this time. Only a few hours left to reach Jerusalem.

But Jesus stops. And approaching the man at the side of the road, He asks what the man wants and needs. Sight, he answers. And the sight is restored.

Further along there is another interruption. A man sits in a tree overlooking the road because he wants to get a view of Christ. He's short, and the crowd is taller by comparison; he's a tax collector, and the crowd is contemptuous of people like him by instinct. No one will give him a break. If he's going to see Jesus, it will be from the limb of a tree.

And as the people pass by, everyone ignores the man in the tree . . . except Christ. Who stops, calls on him to "de-tree," and suggests a conversation. A conversation that infuriates most of the crowd—good Jews do not believe in socializing with tax collectors.

And they are even more outraged when the conversation between Jesus and Zacchaeus is ended. Zacchaeus makes a public announcement. He is sorry for his past practice of extortion and cheating. He will repay what he has unethically taken from others, and he will repay it in multiples of two and four times. The crowd is not impressed, so it seems. Perhaps the people do not believe him.

If they are still angry, Jesus follows with a statement that will make them even more upset: "Today . . . he also is a son of Abraham; for [and here comes Jesus' mission statement] the Son of Man has come to seek and to save that which was lost" (Luke 19:9–10).

Now we know why Jesus would stop and respond to a blind man at the side of the road who shouts for attention, and why He would sit and talk to a tax collector who climbs a tree out of curiosity. Because both are lost, and Jesus was in the business of connecting with such people. People who knew they were lost and who wanted to be found.

And when Jesus went voluntarily to a cross a week later, He was still carrying out that mission. He did His greatest seeking and saving when He died. It fit His mission.

One remembers the night in the Garden of Gethsemane when Jesus wrestled painfully in prayer with the heavenly Father. What was at issue in that agonized moment? The mission. Do we dare speculate that a part of Jesus Christ would have welcomed a reprieve from the mission of the Cross? But what happened in that occasion of prayer was that the mission was reaffirmed in all of its pain and struggle. And He accepted it: "Thy will be done."

If souls drift in a world of seemingly infinite choices and options, in a world of numberless distortions and dissonances, then we Christ-followers are badly in need of some simple covenant between ourselves and the Creator that describes in words not too hard to understand what we believe we are to be and to do.

Some years ago I took this matter of a mission seriously. It came at a time when I was confused about the future. My confusion was driven by a number of things.

A sense of a life in which there was an overabundance of choices to make. Not a thing to complain about, you understand. But the fact remains that there were many good things to do, many organizations to connect with, many people to know and enjoy. There were the opinions of people: persuasive folk, each of whom seemed to have a plan for my life—join us, go there, speak out on this, endorse that, give to. . . .

Then there was uncertainty. Failure had taken its toll; self-confidence was at an all-time low; the future seemed uncertain. And the words of St. Peter in another context echoed through my mind: "What sort of a person ought you to be?"

I was impressed with the words of E. Stanley Jones who wrote,

Man needs nothing so much as he needs something to bring life together into total meaning and total goal. Life for the modern man in East and West needs something to give total meaning to an otherwise fragmented life. He needs an absolute form which he can work down to the relativisms of a day, a master light of all his seeing. He is being pushed and pulled and beckoned to, enticed and bludgeoned from all directions. He is being pushed from relativism to relativism. He is confused—the most confused and yet the most intelligent person that ever existed. He knows everything about life, except how to live it. (Jones, *Kingdom,* p. 11)

My memory went back to the day at the insurance company when I'd been so impressed with the people who knew the business of the company. To the times when I'd sat with people figuring out the business of our congregation. And I found myself saying, What is my business? Good question. A confused soul offers no guidance.

Those sorts of thoughts caused me to seek a fresh understanding of my mission. Some might better understand what I was thinking if I used the word *call* for a moment. What was my call? Or better yet, what was the vocation that my Creator had given me? Can it be reduced to a simple statement, as clear and challenging as the business statement I'd first heard in the office of a company president? Could it be constructed so that one could memorize it, brood on it each day, drive it through a schedule so that even the smallest details of life took on meaning because of it?

And would this encapsulation of my personal vocation be powerful enough that it could carry me in tough times as well as not-so-tough times? Could it be motivational enough that when circumstances conspired to draw me in other directions or when they tempted me to back down because of pressure, I would plow straight ahead—because I knew my "business"?

This, it seems to me, is what Jesus Christ was wrestling through in the Garden of Gethsemane. Some will quarrel with my reasoning. But I suggest that He was clearly seeking reinforcement from the Father, and the issue was His mission. "Seek and save the lost?" Do it on the cross? What was Jesus praying about? If anything, He was asking that the Father drive the mission—"to seek and to save the lost"—deeper into His soul (if that were possible).

One wants to reach out for the metaphor of a battery being charged with current that overflows. Because once on the cross when everything goes wild—the pain, the crowds, the outrageous insults—when everything seems to go on automatic, only what's in the soul will count.

One almost hears Jesus Christ saying to the Father: speak to Me once more of the mission, affirm it once more, let My soul hear the mission one more time. Then the final submission: Thy will be done.

So with Paul. Why travel those innumerable miles marked with shipwrecks, scourgings, hunger, cold, anxiety, stones, threatenings? Why entertain a weakness so great that it invites sickness, depression, loneliness beyond belief? Because of the mission. One hears Paul cry out to God: speak to me of the mission. "To warn every person and teach every person in order to present each person in Christlikeness." And the mission is reaffirmed.

This business of developing a mission is not new and modern. I've already said that in terms of biblical people such as Ezra and Paul. Over the centuries all sorts of men and women have shown themselves to be mission-driven. "There's a tremendous satisfaction in losing your own identity in something that is much more important than you are," Kingman Brewster (one-time president of Yale) once said. And history is marked with people who acted on that principle.

St. Francis, Martin Luther, William Wilberforce (to reform the manners and morals of England), Martin Luther King, Jr. They were all mission-driven. Malcolm Muggeridge thought this way:

> I have a longing past conveying to stay, during such time as remains to me in this world, with the reality of Christ, and to use whatever gifts of persuasion I may have to induce others to see that they must at all costs hold on to that reality; lash themselves to it, as in the old days of sail, sailors would lash themselves to the mast when storms blew up and the seas were rough. For, indeed, without a doubt, storms and rough seas lie ahead. (*Christ and Media*, p. 43)

The great twentieth-century spiritual leader Samuel Shoemaker, who played a significant role in the development of Alcoholics Anonymous, seems to have been telling us something of his mission when he wrote,

> I stand by the door,
> I neither go too far in, nor stay too far out,
> The door is the most important door in the world—
> It is the door through which men walk when they
>      find God.

There's no use by going way inside, and staying there,
When so many are still outside and they, as much as I,
Crave to know where the door is.
. . . The most tremendous thing in the world
Is for men to find that door—the door to God.
The most important thing any man can do
Is to take hold of one of those blind, groping hands.
And put it on the latch—the latch that only clicks
And opens to man's own touch.
. . . So I stand by the door and wait.
For those who seek it.
"I'd rather be a door-keeper . . ."       So I stand by the door.


As I once set about to construct a mission, I asked myself
what the "architecture" of such a statement might include. I came
to these conclusions:

*First, my mission should take into account a life of holiness
that reflects the honor and the character of God.* The person who
seeks a condition of soul in which there is connection with heaven
cannot avoid the biblical call to reflect God's being.

The writer of the Psalms wrote of all creation. Its mission, he
said, was to declare the glory of God. There was nothing made in
creation that was not meant to do this. Even human beings. But
humanity rejected the mission early on in the game of history
through disobedience. Ever since the story has been a bad one.
Everything humanity in its rebellious mood has chosen to do has
not declared the glory of God; rather, the attempt has been to set
forth the honor of humanity. It hasn't worked.

What's worse, everything humanity seems to touch stops declaring the glory of God also. We now have an earth so polluted and
tainted with the afterglow of humanity's exploitation that it becomes
increasingly difficult to find anything that smacks of the original
purposes of creation. Thankfully, some realize this and are doing

something to reclaim the earth for the purposes of beauty, if not sheer survival. The person who organizes his or her life about the Bible might join in this effort, but for a higher purpose: that of reconciling creation to its original purpose—declaring the glory of God.

Just as creation has this mission—declaring the glory—so must a person whose heart seeks after God. It's done through the development of character, or Christlike personhood. As the stars and other heavenly bodies shine to the glory of God, so the follower of Christ chooses to shine with that quality called holiness: focusing on Christ until His nature blends with ours.

*A second item a mission might include is a mandate to be committed to justice and service to one's generation.* Ponderous words for some. The philosophers of business like to speak of something that adds value to a product or a process. A mission ought to reflect a value-added principle. Value added to our generation in the name of Jesus.

Justice speaks of participating in something that either ensures the well-being of others or moves to correct a situation that denies others' well-being. Any reader of the Bible is quite aware that both Testaments are replete with calls for justice in every generation.

Service speaks to the question of where I will invest my skills and gifts in the betterment of my generation. The challenge of service causes me to avoid the trap or habit of going through life as a "taker" and not a "giver."

*Third, my mission must involve something of direct testimony to the character and redemptive work of Jesus and His power to rescue people from the captivities of evil.* Traditionally, this has been called evangelism—the proclamation of the good news of the gospel.

This is a most worthy element in anyone's mission. It was made clear to the disciples by Jesus that the Christ-following life was a life of witness and disciple making. Unfortunately, in our modern zeal we have reduced this to campaigns and programs, and I fear that the downside of that attempt has been to make many feel that witness to Christ is something of an option or, at least, something that lies as a responsibility in the hands of "professionals."

During the years that Gail and I lived in New York City, we made a host of friends, more friends than at any other time in our lives. We learned that the city is not a cold place if one chooses to be a warm person. We also learned that New York certainly has its problems—but one of them is not finding friends of all the cultures and races.

We include among our most special friends a number of men and women who drove the shuttle buses up and down Roosevelt Island, a long finger-shaped island in the middle of the East River under the Queensboro Bridge. We lived in an apartment on the island, and each morning and evening we would take the buses to the tramway that lifted us up and over the river to Manhattan.

Our bus-driver friends came to have breakfast with us on a few occasions. Those who came were all Christ-followers, and our camaraderie with them was strong. One day an interesting conversation took place.

"You sure have an interesting job, Gordon," one of our guests said. "You travel a lot, seem to know a lot of people, always appear to be enjoying yourself."

"I couldn't be happier," I responded.

"Well, your job is a lot better than ours. You help people. All we do is drive these dumb buses up and down the island. What a life!"

I thought about that for several minutes as the conversation went in other directions. And then I said, "I have an idea for all of you."

"What's that?"

"Look, I believe that God will make any job interesting if we believe He wants to use us. Now here's what I suggest. Tomorrow morning before anyone gets on your buses, close the door, face all the empty seats, and say loudly, 'In the name of Jesus, I declare this bus a sanctuary for the next eight hours. And I declare that all the people who enter this sanctuary will experience the love of Christ through me whether they realize it or not.'"

The drivers looked at me as if I was crazy. New York buses as sanctuaries? Then someone said, "I could do that." And others followed, "Me, too."

So for the next few weeks, anytime Gail and I boarded a Roosevelt Island shuttle bus and saw that the driver was one of our friends, we'd lean over and whisper, "You driving a bus or a sanctuary today?"

And the answer usually came back with a grin: "A sanctuary, man, a sanctuary."

A few months later one of the drivers and I met early in the morning and had a chance to talk.

"Do you know that you've changed my life?" he said.

"How's that?"

"Well, you know, this sanctuary stuff. I've been doing it. And it works. Each day I've been turning my bus into a sanctuary, and it's made all the difference in the way I do my job. Why, the other day a guy got on my bus, and he was so mad at me because I wouldn't let him off at a stop that was illegal. He cussed me out something awful. And you know? There was a day when I think I would have gotten up and let him have it. But not in a sanctuary."

"So what happened?"

"I let him off at the next stop and said, 'Hope you have a good day, sir. Nice having you aboard.' And a lady behind me said, 'Charlie, how can you be so nice to a jerk like that?' I just muttered to myself that it wasn't hard if you were driving a sanctuary and not a bus."

I have told that story many times since it happened. People come up later to tell me that they can do it, too. One man I met now flies sanctuaries instead of 747s for Delta Airlines. Another, a trauma surgeon, operates in a sanctuary, not an operating room. They are taking their first steps into the mission-oriented life.

And once you have a mission you are ready to live out of the soul.

*A fourth thought about missions. Some may be surprised if I suggest that a mission ought, somewhere, to express concern and responsibilities for what I like to call the harmonies of creation.* The call of God to Adam and Eve was a proffered mission statement: be fruitful; multiply; have dominion over the earth. We do not have much of a description of what they did with that mission with the possible exception of the naming of the animals (and there must be much more implied in that activity than we're so far figuring out).

But that mission—once given to the first generation—is not a dead one. I have sorrow that the tradition into which I was born has paid little attention to that mission or seen little responsibility to explore what the mission was all about and whether or not it is still operational. I choose to believe it is. And it makes me see the world, the environment, the systems of creation as something for which I have a continuing responsibility.

Perhaps a reconciling responsibility. To do what I can to restore at least a little part of a ruined creation back to its original mission: that of declaring the glory of God.

When our two children—Mark and Kristen—were still of single-digit age, we took them to Canada for a wilderness canoeing trip. We put our canoe and all of its equipment into the water and paddled off into a lake and river system, away from all other people for several days. Somewhere along the waterway we found a small island and made camp. Soon we were enjoying our own private island so much that no one wanted to break camp and keep going. So we stayed.

But soon we noticed that we'd not been the first people to visit the island. Others had been there, and their witness was the many plastic bottles, beer cans, and other refuse that had been left behind.

"I have an idea," Gail said to us one morning. "Let's divide our island into four parts, and each of us will take a garbage bag [we had several with us] and clean up our section. And then we can say that we've given the island back to God, and it can be beautiful for Him again."

We all set out with our bags, and soon the island—a very small island as I said—was clean of all man-made products. It was restored to its original pristine condition. When we had our bags filled and secured, we tied them to heavy rocks and sank them out in the deepest part of the lake. Some environmentalist will wince at this, but he or she must know that we were too far from home base and were ill-equipped to "carry out the litter" we'd collected.

Having restored our island to its beauty and having disposed of the "sin" of earlier visitors, we had our family worship and reconsecrated the island to the glory of God. I've never forgotten that moment. It was a simple act, but it symbolized something that I believe we are called to do. Being concerned for the harmonies of creation, releasing them to once again praise the glory of God.

Finally, *if there is one more thing a mission statement ought to include, it is something about one's—I call it—devotion to God. Devoted* is the word the Old Testament men loved to use when describing one's ultimate passion for someone or something. To be devoted is to turn one's deepest desire toward pleasing and honoring something or someone else. Embedded in the word *devotion* is a promise of loyalty and faithfulness, a bond that will not be broken.

It is no small thing to say, "I am devoted to the God of the Bible and to His Son, Jesus Christ." But these are the words of one who has organized his or her life about the Bible and found in it the God who redeems the repentant person and restores him or her to fullness of life.

And so I learned from the lesson of my friend the company president. If his company needed a mission in order to bring its people together in pursuit of the right objectives, and if Ezra, Paul, Moses, and Jesus thought enough of their work to put it in descriptive form, I should do it, too.

And so several years ago I began to write a short, concise description of what I believed God wanted me to be and to do as a man who called himself a Christ-follower. I discovered that the task was not easy. It took many months before I was prepared to even share it with my wife, Gail. And I discovered, the more I pondered it, used it as an expression of the inclination of my soul, the more I had to keep going back and refining it until I was confident that I had described as precisely as I could what I heard God saying in the depths of my soul.

Every year the mission has gone through review and revision. Today it reads as follows:

> My life-mission is to devote myself to my Creator and to His purposes and to be a faithful follower of Jesus His Son. Additionally, my mission is to pursue order and vitality in my interior world so that the convictions and actions of my life are rooted in my soul and not in the external world around me. And finally my mission is to serve people in the name of Jesus as a generative (seed-planting) man who cultivates hope, wisdom, courage, solidarity, service, and spiritual perspective.
>
> This mission shall be achieved only . . .

- BY COMMUNING WITH GOD through worship, praise, and curiosity. By living in obedience to His will and taking seriously the pursuit of personal holiness and kingdom-building (Pss. 1:1-2; 9:1-2; 19:1, 14).

- BY FOLLOWING AND HONORING JESUS in the development of my values, choices, gifts, capacities, and personal performance. By pushing myself to be a man of Christlike character and wisdom.

- BY INVITING THE SPIRIT OF GOD to empower me so that anyone I encounter and anyplace where I am present become influenced by the reality and liberating power of the kingdom of God.

- BY LISTENING CAREFULLY to my deepest self, hearing the glorious, wordless messages of creation, and absorbing the lessons and questions of history handed down from my "fathers" and all others who have given evidence that they have sought after God.

- BY ORGANIZING MY LIFE AND ITS ROLES according to biblical perspectives.

As for you, my son, . . . know the God of your father, and serve Him with a loyal heart and with a willing mind; for the LORD searches all hearts and understands all the intent of the thoughts. If you seek Him, He will be found by you; but if you forsake Him, He will cast you off forever (1 Chron. 28:9).

As I begin each day, I reread my mission and ask God for the grace and power to fulfill it. The words are lofty; the ideals are almost beyond one's reality. But that's what is good about a mission. It stretches you, and it lets you make no mistake about where you are going.

Living out of the soul demands something like this. Many will be the missions that come from a mind that calculates how to amass fortunes, pursue power, gain notoriety. But here and there a mission will concern itself with what is below the waterline—at soul-level. And the mission will ultimately focus on one thing: pursuing the life God blesses.

# A BEAUTIFUL SOUL

*He taught me . . . that the man who*
*will keep right to the end of the*
*chapter is the man whose gaze is fixed*
*on God, whose joy is in God's*
*company and whose heart is pure in*
*its devotion to the will of God.*
*—George Young, missionary*
*apprentice to George Hunter*

"SHE HAS A beautiful soul," I heard someone say about another. And I wondered to myself: What causes one to use that kind of language to describe something that cannot be seen?

Clearly, the word *beautiful* is being used in a different frame of reference. It's not the same way we might use *beautiful* if we were referring to a physically attractive person. And it is not what we mean when we use the word to describe an object, scenery, or a song. Yet we do not resist what the speaker is trying to say, for we know that we're hearing something about quality of person. We may think to ourselves that this is what one says about someone called a saint.

Let me say the obvious: to have a beautiful soul has nothing to do with where one works or where one lives. Nothing to do with family, race, gender, physical agility, achievement, age, nationality, or intellect. Interesting! Because these are most of the categories by which we usually describe people and evaluate them.

We would naturally think that beautiful souls are the possession of the old, and there is reason for this assumption. Beautiful souls are not normally the possession of those who are young. But I can think of exceptions.

Sometimes children appear to have beautiful souls. My grandchildren, for example. Oh, and other people's grandchildren, too. Seriously, there is beauty in a child's soul. And it is why Jesus was drawn to the children and they to Him, why He would say that the kingdom is not open to anyone who does not enter as a child.

Children have an innocence of soul. They are open, honest, trusting, and believing. They are not cynical, not often despondent, not ambitious to the point of destructive competition. So if one wants to see one version of a beautiful soul, the study of children might not be a bad option with which to begin.

When I review the people who, in my opinion, have beautiful souls, one, a young man, stands high on the list. If the child's soul is beautiful because of its innocence, the man I have in mind seemed to have a beautiful soul because he had been purified through suffering.

I'm thinking of a black South African, an official high in the African National Congress. I met him only once, but the meeting was long enough and provocative enough that I shall never forget him.

Our private visit lasted for only a couple of hours. We spoke, first, of the political realities not only in South Africa but, it seemed, in all Africa. I was impressed with his ability to view the history of our century in broad, sweeping terms, to describe where he saw the nations moving as massive political winds shifted.

When we moved to his own people and their struggle against apartheid, I was once again moved with his understanding of the issues and what it would take to bring about a reversal in the way the races had lived together for most of the past century. His words were punctuated with sadness, determination, optimism, and righteous anger.

When he spoke of what the future could be like, I knew I was listening to a man who was prepared to lay his life on the line without hesitation if it would advance the cause of equity and justice in South Africa. Finally, when he spoke out of his Christ-following faith, I sensed depth and gentleness, heard mercy and forgiveness, felt compassion and urgency. I am not exaggerating when I say that I was astonished. I could not remember meeting such a man as this.

There came a moment when the conversation reached a natural pause, and I said, "Where did you get your training?" Frankly, I thought I would hear Harvard, Oxford, or the Sorbonne. Perhaps I'd hear him say that he had a Ph.D. or an MBA or that he'd been a "fellow" at some world-renowned think tank. But instead there were a smile and a quiet reply that I could hardly hear.

*"I trained on Robben Island,"* he said. I emphasize the quietness of this answer. It was spoken neither boastfully nor triumphantly. It was simply laid out there in the conversation in response to my question. I had the impression that, if I had not asked, he would never have volunteered the information.

Robben Island was the offshore (Alcatraz-like) prison camp where black South African leaders were usually sent during the years when the white-dominated government tried to suppress all opponents of apartheid. For more than a score of years, Nelson Mandela was Robben Island's most famous prisoner.

"You were with Mandela?" I said, trying hard to disguise my shock.

"Five years. He was in the cell next to mine."

"Forgive my curiosity," I said. "But would you mind telling me just a few things about your experience?"

"Not at all." Again the smile. "Every few years the government would search out and jail all the young black leaders. They would sweep them out of sight and eventually dump them out on

Robben Island. But for us it was a profitable strategy. Because that was where we got our education. From Mandela and the others."

I had to ask more questions, and the first was a simple one: "What do you remember most about those days?"

"Remember most? Learning how to forgive! You see, all of us who came to Robben Island came straight from school. We were angry; we were ready to kill the white man, any white man. In prison we lost our names; we were only numbers to the guards. And they kept their guns pointed at us all the time. Each morning we marched out the gate to the rock quarry, and in the evening we marched back. The days always belonged to the guards.

"But the nights were different. The nights belonged to us. During the evening, we who were young sat with the old men. And we listened while they taught us their histories, their tribal languages, their dreams for the black person in South Africa. But most important, Mandela taught us that you can never accomplish anything as long as you hate your enemy. Hate his politics; hate the evil behind those politics; hate the policies that put you in prison. But never hate the person. It takes your strength away."

"You stopped hating?" I said.

"Not right away. It took me almost five years to forgive . . . five years of learning with the old men. But when I did forgive, I was a different person. I knew I had forgiven when I could go to holy Communion on Friday and invite the guard to lay down his gun, come and receive the sacrament with me. So that's the answer to your question. That's where I got my training."

When I left this man's office, I chose to walk to my next appointment rather than to seek more convenient transportation. I knew I had to think about what I'd heard and seen in this conversation. I found myself saying aloud to no one in particular, "I would like to be like that man. To have his sense of focus, his quality of grace, his calmness of heart." I sought to emulate a man fifteen years my junior.

And then it hit me. What I so powerfully envied had come from Robben Island. At the very least I'd have to spend five years on Robben Island to become like him, maybe much longer. The price: five years of doing hard labor, being a number, living under the gun, being deprived of hope from outside sources. Then maybe I might have this character, this beauty of soul that I'd just seen. For when support comes from nowhere else, the soul swings into motion and begins to become what it was meant to be: a place for God to dwell, a place that produces amazing resiliency and grace.

St. Paul, no stranger to this kind of suffering, wrote, "We also glory in tribulations, knowing that tribulation produces perseverance; and perseverance, character; and character, hope" (Rom. 5:3–4). What I had seen in this man was borne out in Paul's observation.

I couldn't help recalling a conversation just days before with another black South African, a pastor who was nearly my age. He had come forward in response to an invitation I'd given at the end of a sermon. "Come," I'd said, "if you need prayer for spiritual renewal and strength." And he had come, embraced me, and begun to weep.

When he regained his composure, he said, "I'm so angry. I've hated the whites for thirty-five years. My heart is so clogged up with bitterness. I don't love my wife as I ought; I can't preach as I should; I can't even say a decent prayer to God. I need to be set free."

When we could talk further, he spoke of a memory from his sixteenth year. He and his parents had stopped at a gas station in a small South African town. He sought a men's room, and finding one and seeing no sign that would prohibit his using it, he went in. But a few minutes later a white man entered and immediately demanded, "What are you doing in here?"

"I said, 'The sign said MEN; it didn't say anything else.'" The pastor began to sob, his whole body shaking as he spoke the next words slowly for the sake of emphasis. "The white man grabbed me and threw me out the door before I was through relieving myself. And as he pushed me out the door, he shouted, 'You're not a man; you're an animal.' I've never been the same since. All my life since then, I've heard those words: 'You're an animal; you're an animal.'"

For thirty-five years the man's soul had known virtually no expansion. Rather than being a glorious and unlimited dwelling place for God, it could be likened to a cramped, rat-infested apartment with no light—not a pleasant place for God to be.

We must do soul work relentlessly. Soul work involves the work of frequent cleansing and the work of frequent refurbishing.

It should not be overlooked that among the very first words we heard Jesus speak when He launched His public work of teaching and disciple making was the word *repent*. A word often associated with revivalism, it is among the most important in all the biblical vocabulary.

Repent carries with it the act of opening the soul and naming what is found. This is not a happy experience for the best of us. Like opening the door to a subbasement in which trash has been permitted to accumulate, opening the soul may expose much of what is supremely unattractive. No wonder most of us find it convenient to put the soul under lock and key.

Repent means to acknowledge this mess in which we continually find ourselves and to seek something new. Repent means to turn away from old ways and attitudes, to embrace new ones. And it seems to me, repent suggests a humbled demeanor before God—a quiet, unresisting disposition that utters the prayer of the old spiritual masters: *Have mercy upon me, for I have sinned.*

I have come to think of the soul as possessing a massive archive, a library of past events and attitudes. In this archive are those roots of motive and direction that must be placed in the light of day, examined as to their health and well-being. And a search of the archive probably involves questions. Hard, sometimes harsh questions that spare nothing.

Somewhere the old spiritual master Meister Eckehart wrote, "The spiritual life has much more to do with subtraction than it does with addition." The questions initiate the subtraction.

To get Cain, one of two sons in the Bible's first family, to face the reality of the darkness of his soul, God asked him, "Why are you angry? And why has your countenance fallen?" (Gen. 4:6).

God asked a depressed and disappointed Elijah who had fled to the desert, "What are you doing here?" (1 Kings 19:9). Jesus asked Judas in the garden, "Friend, why have you come?" (Matt. 26:50). Peter, over a charcoal fire, "Do you love Me more than these?" (John 21:15). And to Saul of Tarsus on the Damascus road, "Why are you persecuting Me?" (Acts 9:4). *Thought questions:* targeted not at the mind but at the soul. As if one were being told: look at yourself, look deep into yourself. For once in your life go below the waterline; search the soul. What is there and why is it driving your attitudes and actions? Questions! Hard, hard questions that, in God's presence, cannot be avoided by taking some version of the Fifth Amendment.

I've found several questions to be helpful when I venture below my personal waterline, into the soul's archive. These are the kinds of questions I imagine Jesus asking in personal conversation with people like myself.

## 1. Who Am I Really Trying to Please?

This is the first of the questions. And it centers on the issue of whose good opinion we find most important to cultivate.

We were made to live to please God. The soul is never more functional than when its entire focus is upon the pleasure of God.

Praise the LORD, O my soul;
> all my inmost being, praise his holy name.
Praise the LORD, O my soul,
> and forget not all his benefits (Ps. 103:1–2 NIV).

This is the soul in motion seeking the pleasure of its Maker. But the evil that lies at the bottom of the soul often causes human beings to lower their sights and aim at other kinds of approval. We begin to expend enormous energies seeking the approval of substitute gods. The entertainer seeks the approval of the audience, the workaholic pursues the approval of the father who never gave him a sense of value for what he was, and the athlete seeks the approval signified by the gold medal or the higher paying contract.

Most of us are not in these categories, but we are all prone to pursue similar or parallel approvals. We want to know that there is someone who is pleased with us, who will stamp value upon us because of what we are and what we have accomplished.

In truth, these are all echoes of the greater approval the soul is designed to seek from God. And when the soul is denied this pursuit—to "praise the LORD, O my soul"—it surrenders the effort to please to other parts of the person. The result is usually a very unhappy one.

When I have the opportunity to speak to an audience of men, I frequently speak of this need to please. For men find it very important to please someone. I recall for them the words of God the heavenly Father to His Son, Jesus, on a couple of occasions: "You are My beloved Son, in whom I am well pleased" (Mark 1:11). At a later date, Jesus would hear the words of His Father: "This is My beloved Son. Hear Him!" (Luke 9:35). These latter words being spoken not only to Jesus but to three of His disciples: Peter, James, and John.

As I relate these affirmations that moved from Father to Son, I say to men, "Is there anyone here in this room who would not cut off his right arm to hear his father say this to him? 'You're my son. I love you. I'm delighted with you.' And to hear him say to others, 'My son knows what he's talking about: *listen to him.*'" The room in which I am speaking *always* becomes intensely silent; heads nod, and not a few eyes glisten. Most of us men know what it is to go through life and never feel that we have earned the pleasure of our fathers. Or it may be the pleasure of a mother or that of a mentor or significant person on our personal horizon.

The soul within a person who lives to please someone less than God is a diminished soul. It is not that there should be no attempt to please others, but that level of pleasing always comes second, as a result of the first.

## 2. What Needs Am I Trying to Meet? What Insecurities Am I Pampering? And What Feelings Am I Storing Up?

These questions make up the second query that one must take below the waterline.

Books—by the scores—are written on these questions every year. An entire industry has arisen in the last years dedicated to helping people surface these underlying currents of need, fear, insecurity, feeling. And people pay good money to visit with therapists on a weekly (and even twice-weekly) basis to gain assistance in exploring the subbasements of life. Here and there one hears a good report of this kind of activity. But I'm not sure that the good reports outnumber the less-than-good ones.

With this industry has grown the theme of victimization. All of these things within me are the result of someone else's injustice perpetrated upon me. And from all of this comes the effort of the support and recovery group movement, an admirable thing to be sure. But not so admirable *if* it conveys to people the notion that we are safe and healthy if we can lay all of our problems at the feet of others: blame them, vent our anger at them, sue them. Then of course the logic suggests that they (whoever the "they" is) should in turn blame someone else. In something of a reverse relay race, we are all seeking to pass the baton of blame and accountability to someone far back and out of sight.

Enough writers and lecturers have helped us explore the extent to which this kind of assigning blameworthiness is necessary. But it may not have helped! Perhaps one might consider an alternative: *forgiving the perpetrator* and turning back to oneself and renouncing the patterns that make one become need-driven.

Deep below the personal waterline, the soul springs into a revitalized perspective when one names the needs, names the insecurities, names the feelings (be they resentment, fear, or anger), and then declares in the powerful name of Jesus that it is time to get beyond them. To embrace new patterns of behavior and conviction. To declare that one will walk in new ways modeled by Christ even if the first steps are tentative, painful, and quite risky.

I am suggesting a new element of toughness directed toward others. A self-directed rebuke that says, "Enough! I am not going to permit myself to be disabled by events noted in my archives. They are of past-history; they shall not be future-history."

Samuel Logan Brengle was a great evangelistic preacher in his generation. He wore the uniform of the Salvation Army. His was a beautiful soul. And part of the reason was his disciplines below the waterline. He would not abide any feelings or insecurities to bind him for long even though, for most of his life, he battled a proneness to depression brought on by an injury to his head when a homeless man hit him with a brick.

His biographer notes a prayer of Brengle's from his diary:

Keep me, O Lord, from waxing mentally and spiritually dull and
stupid. Help me to keep the physical, mental, and spiritual fiber
of the athlete, of the man who denies himself daily and takes up
his cross and follows Thee. Give me good success in my work,
but hide pride from me. Save me from the self-complacency
that so frequently accompanies success and prosperity. Save me
from the spirit of sloth, of self-indulgence, as physical infirmities
and decay creep upon me.

Brengle's biographer, commenting on the prayer, writes,

Thus praying daily and hourly, the prophet kept his passions hot
and his eye single, even as he came down the decline.

Joseph of Egypt models this kind of thinking for us. Smoth-
ered by his father, resented and rejected by his brothers,
dehumanized (at first) as a slave, falsely accused and imprisoned as
an attempted rapist, and forgotten by those whom he tried to serve
beneficially, Joseph had every reason one can think of to drift into a
psychic paralysis, shrivel up, and die.

If any man had the right to a catalog of unmet needs, powerful
insecurities, and feelings of resentment and anger, it was this man.
What is there about Joseph that caused him to renounce the "right"
to wallow in the scandals of his personal archive?

The Bible offers no psychological analysis. It does, however,
reveal something of the man's perspective below the waterline when
he stands face-to-face with his brothers in a dream-fulfilling moment. They have bowed down before him, weeping for fear that
they will lose their lives for actions in the past. Then they had the
power; now he has it.

But Joseph speaks out of a deep soul, from far below the
waterline:

Do not be afraid, for am I in the place of God? But as for you, you meant evil against me; but God meant it for good, in order to bring it about as it is this day, to save many people alive. Now therefore, do not be afraid; I will provide for you and your little ones (Gen. 50:19–21).

The text of Scripture concludes with this: "And he comforted them and spoke kindly to them" (Gen. 50:21).

Centuries later Jesus Himself would hang on the cross, look down upon a spiteful crowd, and say, *Father, forgive them; they don't know what they're doing.*

Today there would be advisors who would say to both Joseph and Jesus, "You would be healthier if you screamed, punished, and transferred your anger over to your victimizers." But the Bible offers an alternative (less expensive, by the way) when it proposes that we renounce the hold of our feelings and anxieties through forgiveness and mercy giving.

Not to do this is to lose whatever weight does exist below the waterline. In Shakespeare's *Richard III*, the title character is unusually ugly because of physical deformation. The evil in his actions he justifies because of his misfortune.

> I, that am . . .
> Cheated of feature by dissembling Nature,
> Deform'd, unfinish'd, sent before my time
> Into this breathing world, scarce half-made up,
> And that so lamely and unfashionable
> That dogs bark at me as I halt by them—
> Why, I . . .
> Have no delight to pass away the time. . . .
> And therefore, *since I cannot prove a lover*
> To entertain these fair well-spoken days,
> *I am determined to prove a villain*
> And hate the idle pleasure of these days. (emphasis mine)

These are the words of a man bereft of his keel. He seems to have no soul.

### 3. With Whom/What Am I Competing?

The soul cannot be healthy when one compares himself or herself to others. The soul dies a bit every time it is involved in a lifestyle that competes. It gives way to the destructive forces of rivalry, envy, and jealousy.

Oscar Wilde told this meaningful story:

> The devil was once crossing the Libyan desert, and he came upon a spot where a number of small fiends were tormenting a holy hermit. The sainted man easily shook off their evil suggestions. The devil watched their failure, and then he stepped forward to give them a lesson. 'What you do is too crude,' he said. 'Permit me for one moment.' With that he whispered to the holy man, 'Your brother has just been made Bishop of Alexandria.' A scowl of malignant jealousy at once clouded the serene face of the hermit. 'That,' said the devil to his imps, 'is the sort of thing which I should recommend.'

I have never known a person in my life with whom I would like to have exchanged places. But that does not mean that I have not occasionally been driven by the competitive instinct, the desire to race ahead of someone, to look better (even to appear more godly, if it is possible to conceive of such a convoluted temptation) by comparison. On every occasion that I have permitted this kind of thinking to take root within, I have been sharply rebuked sooner or later. Until I have learned that there is no percentage in competing with anyone for greater attention, or reward.

In reading A. B. Bruce's great classic *The Training of the Twelve,* I came across this remarkable insight into human behavior. Bruce refers to the Greek would-be philosopher Alcibiades, who in his younger years was a disciple of Socrates. But he later turned on him and even later betrayed his native city into the hands of its enemies. Of Socrates, Alcibiades once said,

> I experience towards this man alone what no one would believe me capable of, a sense of shame. For I am conscious of an inability to contradict him, and decline to do what he bids me; and when I go away I feel myself overcome by the desire of popular esteem. Therefore I flee from him and avoid him. But when I see him, I am ashamed of my admissions, and often times I would be glad if he ceased to exist among the living; and yet I know well that were that to happen, I should be still more grieved.

In great contrast, however, are the words of F. B. Meyer, a man of beautiful soul, who confessed to a temptation to jealousy when at a conference where G. Campbell Morgan was drawing much larger crowds than he was, "The only way I can conquer my feelings, is to pray for him daily, which I do."

And what shall we say of Francis of Assisi?

> So soon as [St. Francis had] followers, he does not compare himself with his followers, toward whom he might appear as a master; he compares himself more and more with his Master, toward whom he appears only as a servant. (Chesterton, p. 122)

### 4. What Rewards Am I Seeking?

Simon Peter had something of this notion in mind when he listened to Jesus go head on head with a wealthy young inquirer who would like to have been part of Jesus' band. "Sell all you have, give it to the poor, and *then* come and follow Me," Jesus had said (See Mark 10:21).

Simon listened to this conversation and then approached

Jesus. My perception of Simon's question is interpreted through my use of italics: "*We have* left everything to follow You! *What then will there be for us?*" What's the payoff in terms of cash, power, connection?

The rewards men and women seek in a subtle way when they approach Jesus are many and varied. For a lot of us, it's the hope that life will turn out OK. That a marriage will occur or, having occurred, be sustained or healed. That a child will not go bad. That a job will not be lost or that a career will be blessed. That there will be acceptance, love, and admiration.

We deny these motives only to reveal their hiddenness in the moment of loss or defeat. From our mouths often comes admission of anger against God that He has let us down in the face of struggle. And in our blaming we do not realize our tacit admission that we expected God to reward us with these things because we were faithful.

This sort of dynamic is illustrated in Jesus' story of the prodigal son. The younger brother who leaves home is, shall we say, an unmitigated rat. Everyone knows that. The older brother who stays at home appears the far more praiseworthy son. He stays to assist his father in whatever the family business is about. He is the faithful one, the loyal one, the loving one. This is clear to anyone who visits the home during the time when the prodigal is gone.

But something different below the waterline shows when the younger brother returns. He is welcomed by the father but not by the older brother.

The inhospitable brother takes the father aside. "Look," he says to the father in a moment of unrestrained anger, "all these years I've been slaving for you and never disobeyed your orders. Yet you never gave me even a young goat so I could celebrate with my friends. But when this son of yours who has squandered your property with prostitutes comes home, you kill the fattened calf for him!"

And the father responds, "My son, you are always with me, and everything I have is yours." This is/was the reward. And the brother had never seen this. In his moment of anger, he reveals what has festered in his soul all through the years. He'd been reward-driven, and what is revealed is not an attractive sight.

## 5. What Guilt or Shame Might I Be Covering?

If the soul is a repository of events and attitudes in the past that are grievous to a righteous God, it cannot be beautiful. Rather, it becomes a place of disease. And what has been covered up increases like a cancer, poisoning the soul until it virtually destroys it.

In another place and time I have written about all I know concerning the horror of secret-carrying, something with which, for a short while, I was well-acquainted. That hidden welt of deceit that enlarges its territory and becomes a building site for larger, more awful events.

Perhaps we have come to the greatest single cause of loss of vitality in the Christian life. The misunderstanding of the importance of repentance. The secrets must be revealed; the cover-up blown away. One must examine the soul daily and sometimes even submit to the examination of trusted others in spiritual community.

Jonathan Edwards, whom some consider to have been the greatest of all American theologians, notes in his diary on November 22, 1772:

> Considering that by-standers always espy some faults which we
> don't see ourselves, or at least are not so fully sensible of: there
> are many secret workings of corruption which escape our sight,
> and others only are sensible of: resolved therefore, that I will, if

I can by any convenient means, learn what faults others find
in me, or what things they see in me, that appear anyway blame-
worthy, unlovely or unbecoming.

Here is Edwards expressing a deep and broken spirit. And when
we use the word *broken*, we mean a soul that is open and given to
examination.

"Try me . . . and see if there is any wicked way in me," so
wrote the psalmist (Ps. 139:23–24), himself, assuming it to be
David, a practitioner of deceit on a number of occasions. The
broken spirit is one in which the doors and windows of the subbasement are flung open to the searching eyes of a God who is both
judge and redeemer.

Our friends in Alcoholics Anonymous seem to have understood this principle better than anyone else. They begin their
Twelve-Step Affirmation with the words: "We admitted that we were
powerless over alcohol—that our lives had become unmanage-
able."

Although some have caught themselves up in theological
criticism about certain aspects of the twelve steps, they have
perhaps missed the significance of the opening statement. That is
repentance! "This is who I am!" the alcoholic cries out. "I am
opening my inner life and declaring my condition." It is one of
helplessness. The doors of the archive are flung wide.

The soul begins its pilgrimage toward beauty in the face of
questions like these. It is broken open through repentance. The
sunlight of grace and mercy begins to flood in. The sewage of the
past is drained away. Something new is begun each day, a fresh
start. And of such a person one begins to hear the comment: "She
has a beautiful soul."

# WHERE WILL YOU BE?

*God is neither the better if thou praise*
*Him, nor worse if thou disparage*
*Him; but thou, by praising Him that*
*is good, art the better; by disparaging*
*thou art the worse, for He remaineth*
*good as He is.*
—St. Augustine

AMONG MY GREATEST memories of being a father to two wonderful children were the nights when it was my responsibility, or shall I say privilege, to put them to bed. Our daughter, Kristy, was a sensitive child who craved a strong sense of structure in her life, and that was no more evident than in her bedtime rituals.

As she crawled into bed, she insisted on a careful procedure for bringing an end to the day. Sheets and blankets had to be drawn tightly up to her chin with no apparent wrinkles from the foot to the head of the bed. Window shades were pulled down to exactly five inches above the sill.

Kristy had seventeen stuffed animals lined up on the floor against the wall in her room, and each night the first in line (tiger, bear, or dog) was tucked in with her. She was circumspect about this arrangement. It could not be the fifth, the ninth, or the fourteenth animal that came to bed with Kristy, for "that would be unfair to the others, Daddy. Each gets its turn." On a few occasions I tried sneaking one out of the proper order and into her bed. But it didn't work.

After evening prayers, I would kiss our little girl and head for the door. There the bedtime liturgy was no less important. The door was to be shut within six inches so that the hall light could cast a glow into the room . . . but not directly. And as I would slip out the door, there would be this final exchange—almost always word for word:

"Where will you be, Daddy?"

"In the living room with Mom, sweetheart."

"Do you think you'll be staying there until I go to sleep?"

"No doubt about it. You call me if you need me."

"OK. But don't go to sleep until I'm asleep."

"Don't you worry. I love you, honey. Good night."

"I love you, too, Daddy. Good night."

*Where will you be?* This is no small question for a child seeking the reassurance that her father or mother will be within shouting distance; no small question either for one who seeks after the God who has said that He desires to inhabit the soul and that He will always be near.

Moses, liberator of the Hebrews, had his moments of anxiety that are reminiscent of those of my daughter, Kristy. "Who am I," he asked, "that I should go to Pharaoh, and that I should bring the children of Israel out of Egypt?"

God's answer: "I will certainly be with you" (Exod. 3:11–12).

And God gave this solemn assurance to men and women throughout the Bible. "I will be with you," He said. That was the assurance that one need never fear being alone in these great challenges requiring heavy weight below the waterline.

"Mysticism has its pitfalls and its limitations," Rufus Jones the quaker wrote, "but this much is sound and true, that the way to know God is to have an inner heart's experience of Him, *like the experience of the Son*" (emphasis mine).

*The experience of the Son.* It is not difficult to conjure up a picture of Jesus, the Son, during His years of public life. There He was moving from village to village, person to person, need to need. Get close enough to watch and you see a tranquillity of spirit, an economy of movement, and a clarity of purpose that leave you deeply moved. Where do they come from?

Answer: From deep below the waterline, the result of those many hours spent in withdrawal from the noises and distractions of public living. It is a steady rhythm of which the gospel writers often take note. He went out to the hills, they say, or He withdrew to a lonely place. Only rarely do we get a glimpse of what went on during those occasions. Perhaps the great intercessory prayer of John, chapter 17, is a hint of what those moments could have been like: "[My prayer is] that they all may be one, as You, Father, are in Me, and I in You" (v. 21).

It is difficult for us to imagine the purity of connection between God the Father and God the Son. The mind bows in incomprehensibility. It must have been a level of communication that is light-years from anything our imaginations might produce.

But if the content of their communion is beyond us to know, the fact that it occurred is not. For it is in moments like those that Jesus built below the waterline, in the invisible places of His soul. We can assume this because the Lord always emerged from such moments to make key decisions and to move toward places that were clearly part of a heavenly design.

One could conclude that those were moments in which Jesus' mission was affirmed, His sense of direction ascertained, His person and relationship with His Father refreshed. Does it seem strange to say these things about Jesus? Does it impress us that He needed these things as badly as we do?

There is no little significance to the fact that Jesus pursued these intimate encounters with the Father. They demonstrate His hunger for heavenly communion while He was here in His incarnate state. And also of importance is the model of relationship it provides for all of us who seek after the life God blesses. If the Son thought these hours important, what are we to think about their place in our calendars?

The weight we accumulate below the waterline in such times of Jesus-like communion will be the direct result of how we spend that time. If it is merely an event during which one sets forth a list of petitions or requests, the resultant weight of the soul will most likely be inconsequential.

To earn extra money during some of my college and seminary days, I often worked temporary jobs in freight terminals in the city of Denver. One of my favorite assignments was to load trucks at the Keebler cookie factory. There I hoisted large boxes full of cookies that weighed very little. I could fill a truck fast, feel that I had worked hard. And the pay was good. A much better alternative to times I spent at Gates Tire and Rubber.

So when I think of those days, I am reminded of how important it is to weigh the religious acts of a person before daring to make any sort of judgment. We can actually be large boxes with little weight. This is what is liable to happen when our withdrawal times are spent in little more than asking.

The life God blesses is marked by a tenacious desire to acquire an intimate knowledge of who He is. To become aware of nature, His mighty acts, His purposes, and His design for us. This exercise is actually what we call *theology*—the study of God and His purposes.

Most people cringe before the word *theology* because they have this image of a body of information that is complicated and (dare I say it?) irrelevant. Monitor the thoughts of most church-goers, and you will most likely discover that they are glad that a few people on seminary campuses love theology because they do not. Theology seems unpromising to those who think making money, expanding careers, and building a family are what life is about.

And yet theology is at the root of the question: *Where will you be?* We may not be aware of it, but we are immediately dabbling in theology when the disruptive moments come and we ask the why-questions, the what-am-I-to-do questions, the what-does-this-mean questions. We are now on theological ground.

A couple for whom I have deep respect lost a son in a bizarre skiing accident. He was a young man with great promise, and his brother and sister had looked to him with great affection and admiration. And now he is gone. All of them have to make sense of it.

I say to the father who is numb with grief over the loss of his son, "I want you to think about what you're going through during these days. This is a time when God may want to speak with you in very powerful ways. Grieve as you must, but don't let your grief be the kind that will turn you bitter and hard. Let the Father whisper in your ear. Great things may happen to you in this terrible, terrible moment."

Now years later he reminds me that I had said this to him. "You were right," he says. "God did speak to me. Those were the days when I gave my life to Jesus. The loss of my son has been incalculable. But in the midst of my grief Christ came to me, and He changed me forever."

This same couple talks with me just a few days ago. We are not more than ten years past the awful moment when the news had come that their son had died on the ski slopes. "Our whole family is totally different because of his death," they say. "We watch other families we know going through similar kinds of experiences, and all they have is anguish. We miss our son, but we know that in his death he gave us the chance to come to Jesus."

This is what happens when the soul opens its doors first to the questions of the previous chapter and then to the secrets God wishes to whisper about Himself.

What are the theological secrets God may wish to introduce to the builder of weight below the waterline? Over a period of time, I have been able to categorize a host of these secrets into seven parts. The exercise has been helpful because I return to each of the seven on a daily basis and recycle them each week.

I call this set of secrets the liturgy of my soul. By disciplining myself to ponder each secret on a daily basis, I assure that I don't fall into the trap of concentrating on a few familiar things. But I am pressed each week to ponder a large part of the truth that God has revealed about Himself in the Bible.

## Sunday: A Day of Creation and Resurrection

For example, on Sunday morning, my soul welcomes the secrets of the *God who is the Author of life and Creator of the heavens and the earth*.

On the early pages of my journal where I have developed my personal liturgy of worship are these words about Sunday's meditation:

God is my maker: the essence of what I am is good. But the evil in me is foreign tissue. The heavens and the earth are His, and it all—except what humanity has exploited and destroyed—gives evidence to His glory. THIS IS A DAY OF CREATION AND RESURRECTION.

Thus says God the LORD,
Who created the heavens and stretched them out,
Who spread forth the earth and that which comes from it,
Who gives breath to the people on it,
And spirit to those who walk on it:
"I, the LORD, have called You in righteousness,
And will hold Your hand" (Isa. 42:5–6).

This of course is where the Bible begins, *"in the beginning,"* the truth to which the biblical writers return again and again when they ask the question, *Where will you be?* Reassurance and soul-building begin with the reminder that the indwelling God made everything.

The implications stream out from that point. He not only *made* everything, but He is in the process of continually making and sustaining. Creation is not a past event; it is a continuing one. Each human being who comes into the world is an event of creation, and God has breathed into each His own breath.

Creation was not and is not happening purposelessly. The design of all created things is to reflect the glory of God. Listen to Mozart—as I am doing while I write these words—and you may be caused to pause and ponder the genius of the composer. Stand before Rembrandt's great painting the *Night Watch* in the museum at Amsterdam—as I've done—and you are awed by the skill of the painter. And read some of the great novels of Chaim Potok—as I've enjoyed doing—and you are amazed at the skill of the storyteller to draw you up and into the tale. Each of these is a tiny, minute sample of what creation is meant to do. Reflect the majesty, the honor, the glory, the raw power of the Creator.

On Sundays, I think of these great beginnings and this process in which all things and life are generated out of nothing more than the sheer word of God. He spoke and He speaks; and things become, and they function in submission to Him. Oceans and their living creatures, mountains and their canyons, stars, quasars, and all the rest of those strange things astronomers find in space. All this made by Him.

St. Paul spoke of the Creator as One who is to be honored and thanked. The psalmist mused upon creation and marveled that such a God could be interested in humankind in the slightest. The prophet pictured all these created things as singing with joy and clapping their hands. Great poetry! Great lessons of what a Sunday morning in meditation could be like for those who take the time to praise and worship the God who is Lord of everything.

The practical result of such a meditation is my reaffirmation that, having made everything, this God owns everything. My body, my skills, my life force, my material possessions—nothing left out. I am merely a manager of the things He owns.

Sunday then is not only a reminder of His creative genius and energy; it is a blunt recall to the fact that all this stuff I think is mine to use as I please (since I "earned" it) is not mine after all. Private ownership is, in fact, an arrogant myth. If anyone has private ownership, it is this God who lives in heaven and in the soul of the one who is lowly in spirit and open to receiving His indwelling presence.

### Monday: A Day of Glory

But there are six more days of the week, and that brings me to Monday. For on Monday, *I set myself to remembering that there is a kingdom, God's*. My personal liturgy reads,

> God is my King: I am a servant in His kingdom, and I stand before Him today in reverence and holy fear. His kingdom begins in me and in all who bow before Him in submission. THIS IS A DAY OF GLORY.

> Oh, clap your hands, all you peoples!
> Shout to God with the voice of triumph!
> For the LORD Most High is awesome;
> He is a great King over all the earth (Ps. 47:1–2).

Spend time each Monday in converse with the Lord of the kingdom, and one's life and schedule become marked with sacredness. This "Unshakable Kingdom," as E. Stanley Jones once called it, is forever and ever, and we are servants/citizens in it through faith in Jesus the Lord.

Jones, who spent a lifetime preaching the kingdom of God around the world, never lost his enthusiasm for this Monday aspect of my soul-liturgy. Recalling a day many years ago when he was traveling in Iran, he describes a moment when he was snubbed by a French diplomat who, in a difficult moment, might have provided him transportation but refused.

> I suppose I should have felt squelched, but inwardly I straightened up and said to myself: "If he is a French diplomat, then he represents a shaky French kingdom which has had about twenty-six governments in about thirty years. If he is a diplomat, I'm an ambassador of the Unshakable Kingdom which has had one government since the foundation of the world and will have one government to the end of time."

Later the two found themselves aboard a ship on the Caspian Sea. Jones tells the story of what happened:

> On the way . . . the diplomat was caught by a treacherous lock in a bathroom and couldn't get out. So he waved frantically to me and said, "Please sir, extricate me." And the Ambassador extricated the diplomat.

Jones couldn't resist making a point with his story:

> Is that what the ambassadors of the Kingdom must do? Extricate the diplomats of this world who have boxed themselves up in the bathrooms of impossible ways of life and are saying, if they only knew it, "Please sirs, extricate us," and we must humbly say, "Brother, this is the Way, walk ye in it—the way of the Kingdom."

This is what I try to think about on Monday morning. That from the depths of my soul and all the way to the tiniest item on my day's schedule, I will act as a servant, an ambassadorial servant in the kingdom. The One whose pleasure I will seek is Lord of that kingdom. This is theology at its best; this is life in the service of Christ.

### Tuesday: A Day of Accountability and Mourning

Then comes Tuesday. And I think of it as a heavy day for my soul. The subject matter is not pleasant to ponder, but ponder one must. On this day, I must affirm that *God is my judge.*

My journal reads for Tuesday:

God is my judge. Before Him and before Him only do I stand guilty of my sins, justifiably condemned. THIS IS A DAY OF ACCOUNTABILITY AND MOURNING.

O LORD, I know the way of man is not in himself;
It is not in man who walks to direct his own steps.
O LORD, correct me, but with justice;
Not in Your anger, lest You bring me to nothing (Jer. 10:23–24).

As I said, these are not happy thoughts. But necessary ones, nevertheless. If there are not moments of intense sorrow over one's evil, a moment of contrition and repentance, then all other aspects of theology that may be brighter lose their meaning.

God is indeed, and must be, a judge. There are a time and a place for one to feel the heat of His holy anger against all sin. "The wrath [or anger] of God is revealed from heaven against all ungodliness," St. Paul wrote (Rom. 1:18). He would not let his readers bypass this fact with glibness. A message of grace and love should not be used to cover up the horror of the fact that (Paul's words) "in me . . . nothing good dwells" (Rom. 7:18).

One does not hear a lot of preaching, nor is there a landslide of books written these days, on the judgment of God. It is neither a popular subject nor a soothing one. And perhaps that is why it is easy to avoid or downplay in our popular theology. But we downplay it to our regret.

In a time when people were more willing to think and brood on the judgment of God, John Berridge, a great Church of England preacher of the eighteenth century, wrote,

> Ten years ago I hoped to be something long before this time, and seemed in a promising way; but a nearer view of the spiritual wickedness of my heart, and of the spiritual demands of God's laws, has forced me daily to cry, "O wretched man that I am! God be merciful to me a sinner!" I am now sinking from a poor something into a vile nothing; and wish to be nothing that Christ may be all. I am creeping down the ladder from self-complacence to self-abhorrence; and the more I abhor myself, the more I hate sin, which is the cause of that abhorrence.

Don't let Berridge throw you. Almost in knee-jerk fashion we are tempted to respond to words like these and accuse the writer of wallowing in self-made guilt, of making us feel badly about ourselves. Don't we live in a day when positive, self-esteeming things are supposed to be said? Should we not tell ourselves that we are special, that we are loved, that we are victims?

If we wonder where the holy men and women are or why they are in such short supply, it may be instructive to reread Berridge's words. For holy people do not wallow in guilt, nor is their self-esteem in short supply. But there is an honesty of soul in them that many of us would like to avoid. They know all too well that their sins are a grief and an offense to God and therefore also to them. They fear the retribution of a God whose holiness and sense of justice must cause Him to render a guilty verdict upon all who stand before Him in judgment.

Berridge enlarges upon this thought:

As the heart is more washed, we grow more sensible of its remaining defilement; just as we are more displeased with a single spot on a new coat, than with a hundred stains on an old one. The more wicked men grow, the less ashamed they are of themselves; and the more holy men grow, the more they learn to abhor themselves.

This is why I think it important to guarantee myself that at least once a week, I am going to regain touch with the God who is also judge and who does indeed condemn us for our sins. It is not a happy experience, as I've said, but it does make me look forward to Wednesday.

## Wednesday: A Day of Redemption

Wednesday: when the liturgy for my soul centers on the fact that *God Is My Redeemer*. Again the journal:

God is my Redeemer. In Jesus He has provided a way (the atonement of His Son) to satisfy divine justice, and, at the same time, offer me spiritual liberation and adoption into His kingdom-family. THIS IS A DAY OF REDEMPTION.

> Isaiah speaking the words of God:
> "Is My hand shortened at all
>     that it cannot redeem?
> Or have I no power to deliver?" (Isa. 50:2).

> And also: "And the [redeemed] of the
>     LORD shall return,
> And come to Zion with singing,
> With everlasting joy on their heads.
> They shall obtain joy and gladness,
> And sorrow and sighing shall
>     flee away" (Isa. 35:10).

This is a wonderful day for my soul. To pack into it the reminder of a redeeming God removes all the heaviness of the previous day.

As children we were often told, for illustrative purposes, of a courtroom scene. Of a judge who calls for the next case only to discover that his son stands before him accused of a serious auto violation. The evidence is presented, and it is unimpeachable. And when it is time for the verdict, the judge can only say with judicial firmness, "Guilty!"

The judge is not free to overlook the seriousness of his son's offense. He cannot claim family privilege because his loyalty must be to the law and its supreme demand for justice. And so the guilty verdict is pronounced, and with it, the accompanying penalty. A stiff fine.

But then something different happens, the storyteller says. As the defendant is led away to the place where he must pay, the judge leaves his bench, removes his judicial robe, and joins his son at the desk where fines are paid. He is no longer a judge; he is a loving father.

His hand is upon his son's shoulder as he identifies with him and his predicament. Why, he even reaches into his pocket and finds the cash that will help his son fulfill his obligation to the law. Two people have acted here: the man who is judge and the man who is redeemer. A rescue, a redeeming event has happened here. Justice has been properly served and so has love. Both by the same person.

The Greek word for redemption *(agorazo)* is related to the notion of entering a slave market and purchasing a slave for the purpose of setting him free. And on Wednesdays, I am often caused to picture the powerful Jesus entering the marketplace, where I am a slave to the sin that the Father has judged so severely, and setting me free.

This is great theology. It brings relief to the troubled soul; it brings delight. Horatio Spafford wrote a great song in the midst of a terrible personal tragedy more than a hundred years ago. One verse of his song reads,

> My sin—
> Oh, the bliss of this glorious thought,
> My sin—
> Not in part but the whole,
> Is nailed to the Cross,
> And I bear it no more:
> Praise the Lord, praise the Lord,
> O my soul!

And then the simple refrain, one phrase repeated twice:

> It is well with my soul.
> It is well with my soul.

In a world where, it is said, nothing is free, redemption is. Free to the one who moves toward the Cross, kneels, and receives the gift of redemption. On Wednesday, I think about this. And my soul is greatly enlarged. Lightened from the load of yesterday's reminder of deserving judgment. And then given a greater weightiness of grace that comes to the redeemed person: weight below the waterline that stabilizes and assures seaworthiness.

### Thursday: A Day of Provision

On Thursdays, I remind my soul that *God is my shepherd.* This of course was David's great reminder to his soul when he wrote, "The LORD is my shepherd." He was comfortable with the metaphor because he had been one. He knew what it was like to lead, feed, heal, and protect sheep. He had strong memories of staying awake through the night when there were predators in the neighborhood. He knew the responsibility his father had given him to preserve the family assets. Shepherding was serious business.

And he knew how skittish sheep could become if they became separated from the shepherd and felt vulnerable. That, he couldn't afford to let happen. Fight a lion? A bear? With his bare hands if necessary.

> When a lion or a bear came and took a lamb out of the flock, I went out after it and struck it, and delivered the lamb from its mouth; and when it arose against me, I caught it by its beard, and struck and killed it (1 Sam. 17:34–35).

So when David cast about for a word picture to describe what he knew about the God who is Creator, Lord, Judge, and Redeemer, he chose the word *Shepherd*. Everyone in his day knew what shepherds are supposed to do. And so David used a vocational term to develop a theological view of God and what He does when in relationship with those who love to humbly call upon His name.

My journal reads on this morning:

> God is my shepherd. By His Spirit, I have need of nothing else. He provides, protects, feeds, leads. THIS IS A DAY OF PROVISION.
>
> I will sing of the mercies of the LORD forever;
> With my mouth will I make known Your faithfulness to all
>     generations.
> For I have said, "Mercy shall be built up forever;
> Your faithfulness You shall establish in the very heavens"
>     (Ps. 89: 1–2).

This is a time to meditate upon the kindness, the caring nature of God. To fill the soul with those reminders that one indeed may be "sheepish," but our God has been revealed as a faithful shepherd. This is a day to "lighten up."

Somewhere I heard of the time when Cardinal Basil Hume, once the leader of English Roman Catholics, reflected upon his boyhood and his not infrequent attempts to raid the cookie jar in his mother's kitchen. In a stern voice she would protest and warn him that God saw his hand in the cookie jar and would one day be harsh with him. This was hardly an adequate deterrent. Then Hume told his listeners, "Now, today, I half expect that when I someday stand before God, the Lord will raise the subject of the cookie jar and say, 'Basil, why didn't you take two?'"

Hume's God is a kind God. We need this view that David has given us. We need it because it is accurate, just as accurate as is the Tuesday view of God as judge. The judge and the shepherd are just two of the many attributes of the infinite and holy God.

### Friday: A Day of Compassion and Intimacy

On Friday, my journal calls me to reverence the *God who is my Father*. It says,

> God is my Father: He has compassion and tender affection for me, and He offers me a personal relationship as Father and friend.
> THIS IS A DAY OF COMPASSION AND INTIMACY.

> As a father has compassion on his children,
>     so the LORD has compassion on those who fear him;
> for he knows how we are formed,
>     he remembers that we are dust (Ps. 103:13–14 NIV).

I love to think about the God who is Father. Because the father role is the most important one I have ever taken upon myself throughout my life. I know fatherhood: its ups and downs; its successes and failures; its delights (many) and burdens (few).

I know what it's like to sit in the audience and watch my daughter in the lead role of a stage play. I have walked the sidelines of many soccer games and watched my son score winning goals. I have held both in my arms in their moments of supreme disappointment and humiliation. I hold deep in my heart the memories of many conversations where we talked at soul-level about the things that hurt us, draw us, and delight us. This fathering business is a man's greatest gift in life.

And so to hear the Bible speak of God as my Father moves me at the greatest depths of my soul. The word—*Father*—speaks of something deep beyond words. A presence, an empathy, one who steps out just ahead and shows the way.

My father and I have never been in a position to enjoy continued intimacy. But there came a time in my life, just a few years ago, when I needed him more than anything. And he came! We were two men, two ordinary men, when we met in that dark moment in my life. But something, a deep compassion and understanding, leaped from our hearts as we embraced and cried together. His presence at that moment was a reflection of God's presence when He says to us, "I am your Father."

## Saturday: A Day of Hope

The soul-liturgy of the week is almost ended. And it ends on Saturday. This is a day when the soul must be reminded of eternity. That *God is my everlasting life.*

The journal says,

God is my life. Through His gift, I have the promise of everlasting life. Death is a threshold to something incomprehensibly bright and wonderful. The work of eternity will be that of discovering the infinite depths of His glory. Sadness, conflict, brokenness, weakness will be things of the past, not remembered. Worship will be the order of the day. And we shall see Him as He is. THIS IS A DAY OF HOPE.

"Behold, the tabernacle of God is with men, and He will dwell with them, and they shall be His people. God Himself will be with them and be their God. And God will wipe away every tear from their eyes; there shall be no more death, nor sorrow, nor crying. There shall be no more pain, for the former things have passed away." Then He who sat on the throne said, "Behold, I make all things new" (Rev. 21:3–5).

My neighbor's wife was dying of cancer. I was at the hospital with him as we waited for her life to end. It was a difficult moment because she thrashed about in her bed in semiconsciousness. And no medication or medical treatment seemed to bring her a modicum of rest. It was clear to me that the physicians and the nurses had exhausted every means at their disposal to assist her in this dying hour. And it was a difficult thing for them because during her illness they had all come to love her. So their professional poise was affected by emotional attachment.

I am not given to doing this kind of thing, but I felt impelled to ask permission to step to her bedside. In turn the medical personnel surrounding the bed stepped back. It was clear that they welcomed anything that anyone, including a pastor, could do.

I placed both of my hands on J——'s emaciated shoulders, now thinned by the ravages of this terrible ordeal, and I gently pressed her back into her pillow.

"J——," I said, "it's Pastor Mac. Listen to me! Are you listening? Do you hear me?"

She looked at me with eyes that were filled with fear, almost panic. "Yes, Pastor Mac, I hear you."

"J——, I'm going to say something to you, and I want you to listen as carefully as you can. Don't move, don't speak, just listen! OK?"

"Yes, Pastor Mac," she whispered, "I'm listening."

And then I reached deep into my soul for the simplest, most familiar words of the Bible. Words that I now ponder every Thursday when I think of the God who is there. And I said, "The Lord is my shepherd. . . . I have everything that I need. . . . He makes me to lie down in green pastures. . . . He leads me to still waters. . . . He restores my soul. . . . He leads me on paths of righteousness for His name's sake. . . . And even though [and here I paused and repeated myself several times] . . . and even though . . . and even though . . . even though I walk through the valley of death . . . I am not afraid. . . . I have nothing to fear. . . . Do you hear that, J——, nothing to fear . . . because You are with me.

"J——, we've known each other for a lot of years, and we've talked about this moment when any one of us might go to be with Jesus. You're going first, J——. He's a wonderful Shepherd, and He's ready to take good care of you. Do you hear me, J——? He's ready to take good care of you."

I felt the anxiety, the panicky energy, leave her. Her eyes became soft, and she relaxed in her bed. And then I listened as, with a calm voice, she turned to her husband and whispered, calling him by name, "Thank you for being so good to me, for loving me. You've been a good husband, and I love you."

And then J—— looked to her daughter, "Mommy loves you, dearest; be strong for Daddy." And then to the medical personnel who stood there, "Thank you for taking such good care of me; thank you for all you've done. I love you all."

Almost instantly, following those words, J—— closed her eyes and went to sleep. A few moments later she met the Shepherd face-to-face, crossed the threshold of death, and understood for the first time the full meaning of everlasting life.

And that's why we all love to sing with increasing frequency:

> When we've been there ten thousand years,
> Bright shining as the sun,
> We've no less days to sing God's praise
> Than when we'd first begun.

I love to think about the resurrection-God who has promised eternal life. To think about heaven and its glorious work and worship services. I love to think of being reunited with my grandfather Thomas and having conversations with men like Daniel and Barnabas, my biblical heroes. And I want to meet men and women like the hospitable Priscilla and Aquila, Polycarp who told his persecutors that he was prepared to stand against the whole world, and Augustine who was so open and honest about his struggles with sin and his love of grace. How about talks with St. Francis, Mary Slessor the tough missionary of Calabar, Samuel Logan Brengle of the Salvation Army, and Ethel Waters the wonderful singer of gospel songs? And that's just the beginning.

And so that's what Saturday morning is like. Pondering God, the Giver of eternal life, and a future of futures.

The great English parliamentarian William Wilberforce spent a lifetime fighting all the economic forces of the British Empire in his hatred of slavery. If anyone needed a life below the waterline that was properly weighted, it was Wilberforce. And where did the weight come from? He wrote,

> In the calmness of the morning before the mind is heated and weary by the turmoil of the day, you have a season of unusual importance for communion with God and with yourself.

And one of his biographers, Garth Lean, observes,

> In the day to day battle it was more and more these early morning
> hours (kept up in spite of late nights and chronic ill health) and
> his quiet Sundays which gave him strength and perspective on
> himself and the world.

Now theology isn't so bad, is it? This is the theology that fills
the soul with good weight and prepares things below the waterline
for any eventuality. God blesses lives who think about these things.

Our daughter, Kristy, asks, "Daddy, where will you be?" And
I respond, "In the living room, sweetheart, with Mom." And she
sleeps fully assured.

And I am caused to live fully assured. Because when I ask,
"Where will God be?" I have some answers to draw upon from soul-
level. The answers are there because week after week, I've been
packing the truth into the soul, below the waterline.

# CONVICTIONS GROW IN
# SPECIAL SOIL

*God gave him a character of great majesty.*
*—Members of the Geneva Council on John Calvin*

A FEW YEARS ago the federal government decided to sponsor the building of an atomic particle accelerator in Texas. Planners said the enormous and astronomically expensive atom smasher would dwarf any other in the world. It would take us several steps closer, they said, to discovering the secrets of the universe, a claim we frequently hear from the scientific community as it requests its billions of dollars for research.

The particle accelerator was to be built underground, and so with the blessing of government money, construction began on a circular tunnel, which, if it had been completed, would have been several miles in circumference.

But Congress recently had second thoughts about the cost of the particle accelerator, and construction came to a halt. What is now left after the workers have abandoned the job site is a five-mile slightly curved tunnel large enough to accommodate a truck. Problem: the tunnel goes nowhere. You don't want to know how much this part of the tunnel that was supposed to aid in discovering the secrets of the universe has cost.

Now the question arises: Does this tunnel that goes nowhere have any use? Answer: someone thinks so. The tunnel contains the ideal growing conditions, a businessman says, for growing mushrooms. Now some of us must think about this. A multi-multi-multi-million-dollar tunnel built to discover the secrets of the universe will quite likely end up being used as a mushroom farm.

The varieties of mushrooms that most of us like to spread across our salads and dinners have to grow in a very special ambience: a consistently cool temperature, a darkened place, with carefully controlled humidity. Caves are good places; they're relatively inexpensive. And apparently so are tunnels built at great taxpayer expense. Presumably, the country will be awash in mushrooms in a year or two.

If a tunnel is an ideal growing space for mushrooms, the soul is the ideal growing space for something else. We call them *convictions*. A more modern word might be *values*.

Let me propose this notion. Ideas and thoughts emerge from the mind. Feelings from the emotions. But convictions (or values) arise from the soul. What the mind produces is generally the product of a rational process. A good idea or thought can be defended on the basis of evidence or logic.

Feelings, on the other hand, are simply feelings, indicators of how a person is responding to some event or person. One defends thoughts but not feelings. You build the former, and you experience the latter.

Convictions are different. They are principles of life that grow out of the soil of our belief, like mushrooms in the ideal conditions of the tunnel.

When I engage in the liturgies of the soul that I described in a previous chapter, the practical result will be the formation of convictions. The theology that frightens so many of us is not impractical. *It produces "actionable" principles for living*.

If, for example, God is indeed Lord of the kingdom (a theological statement), then the implication is that I am to live as a servant (like it or not), carefully handling the "stuff" placed in my care, mindful that I am accountable for its use. This implication becomes a conviction and therefore a driving force behind my choices and actions on a daily basis.

A simple biblical example of this process might be found in the story of the confrontation Peter and John had with the religious leaders of Jerusalem. When told to stop preaching the gospel of Jesus in the streets of Jerusalem, Peter replied, "Whether it is right in the sight of God to listen to you more than to God, you judge. For we cannot but speak the things which we have seen and heard" (Acts 4:19–20).

The issue for the apostles is one of conviction. There is a determination born in the soil of their souls. It is guiding their choice to speak boldly, and they will not be muzzled by law, by force, by popular opinion. A conviction now drives their performance.

Conviction and character are closely associated concepts. *Character* is a word we use to describe the overall demeanor of a person. It provides a picture of how we see this individual living day in and day out through routine events. And it creates our anticipation of how this person would act in a difficult situation where rules were suspended and one had only the law written in the soul to guide action. But this form of character is the product of convictions, things believed deep within.

I have lived long enough to have assessed something of my own character. To say that it is flawed character is an understatement. Occasionally, I have heard someone speak of another in terms like these. "He has a character flaw," they say. Which is to infer that others do not. All character is flawed. Dig deep enough into anyone's soul, hold the life under intense scrutiny, and you will

find character flaws. And do that with me, and you will find them—
to my everlasting regret.

As I have assessed my own character (if one can actually do
this with any objectivity), I have found moments in which I take
great delight. Such as the time early in our marriage when, while in
graduate school, Gail and I found ourselves in deep financial
difficulty because we had to sell our home but couldn't connect
with a buyer.

During that time of desperation, a businesswoman in real
estate claiming to be a Christian came to us and expressed strong
confidence that she could sell our home for us. With a great sense
of relief we signed the necessary contracts. And to our delight,
within a few weeks she told us that she had a buyer.

But then the fine print emerged. There were special consid-
erations. We would, she said, have to carry a second mortgage (in
other words, lend the buyer some of our money) and enter into some
rather creative agreements to bring the sale about. We, in our
naiveté, agreed. She assured us that we couldn't go wrong, and
since she labeled herself a Christian, we chose to trust her judgment.

It took less than two months for these arrangements to sour.
Second mortgage payments were not made, and what's worse, we
learned that the first mortgage payments were not being paid either.
The mortgage holding company was about to hold Gail and me
accountable and initiate legal actions, which would tarnish our
credit record and eventually cost us large sums of money. Money
that we did not have.

Matters became further complicated when we learned that the
family who had bought our home had broken up. The father had left
the family, and a mother and several children were surviving on
welfare supplements. We had no choice but to find the money to

pay the monthly house payments they had failed to make. In effect, we were paying for the family to live in our home. And that on the income of a graduate student.

When we sought legal advice, we were told the solution was simple. Evict them! Sue them! And that's where the character issue began to emerge. What did we believe? How would we act in this moment? Vindictively? Vengefully? Forcibly?

Our convictions would not permit us to take such drastic steps even though the law was on our side and even though our own resources were meager. We were a young couple in our mid-twenties, but that had been long enough for us both to have grown convictions in the soil of our souls that said that one does not destroy other people in the midst of their hardship—even if the right is yours.

"How often shall my brother sin against me, and I forgive him? Up to seven times?" Simon Peter asked Jesus, thinking himself to be more than noble when he reached the number seven. After all, he was a product of a culture that was vengeance-oriented. An eye for an eye was the order of the day. It was one's right when wronged.

If Peter thought he was being magnanimous with his number seven, he was quickly pushed backward with Jesus' answer. "I do not say to you, up to seven times, but up to seventy times seven" (Matt. 18:21–22). The ultimate number?

What was Christ doing? Planting a conviction in Simon's soul. A conviction that would have to grow (like a mushroom?), be tested, framed occasionally in failure, and then brought to maturity at a later day when it was most needed.

That was what was happening to us. We were being pushed back. The issue became not one of how we could assert our rights in a conflict with a family devastated by marital separation and sudden poverty. The issue was whether or not we could absorb a difficult blow and seek a higher solution. And we chose to do the latter.

Within a few months the matter was resolved. But I must add that it was resolved with the loss of several thousand of our dollars in a time when dollars were worth a lot more than they are today. It took Gail and me several years to recoup our loss, but I do not recall that we ever regretted the experience. It reinforced a conviction within our souls. We have never again had to face a similar situation, but we are both aware that the welfare of people is more important to us than money. We have that conviction, and we've proved to ourselves that we can live by it.

That conviction was the result of our commitment to Monday's theology: that the Lord is King, and that we are servants in His kingdom. Therefore, we will act as servants, and we will put God's interests before our own. Let me pause and add a disclaimer. One should not assume that we have practiced this conviction on a fail-safe basis. No one has. But the conviction is our guide-star, and when we have been tempted to resist the conviction, we know it.

The Western nations are reeling today because generations are growing who show the evidence of almost no convictions. Newspaper editorials, radio talk shows, and public forums are full of voices crying out for someone to do something about violence on the streets, the increasing number of unwed pregnancies, and the neglect of children. The talk is of values: Where are they?

So far education, government programs, and the therapeutic community—said to be the saviors of our modern society—have not been able to do the job of developing the kinds of restraints and positive patterns of life that are supposed to be part of the good life. And that does not surprise anyone who pursues life from a biblical perspective.

Those who have organized their lives about the Bible believe that behavior arises from convictions birthed in the soul. And from the soul come choices and attitudes that benefit everyone and are a glory to God. But secular society scorned that idea several decades ago, and now we are living with the products of their programs.

## How Are Convictions Grown in the Ambience of the Soul?

*We can't ignore the fact that they are usually first modeled by the significant people on the screen of our lives.* These are usually our mothers and fathers, members of our extended family and community. In the stories that are told to us in our most impressionable years. And principles that are taught through song and motion.

In such forms the seeds of conviction are planted in the souls of children where they can take root over the first few years. My own sense is that the growing season for convictions is best in the first seven years. From there on out the growing season of life grows more and more difficult to control.

Some may disagree, but I know of no better way to open the soul and pour in the seeds of conviction than with the use of music. If generosity is a conviction in the lives of the adult children in our family, it probably goes back to the fact that in the earliest months of their lives, their mother was singing to them. "A Sharing Time Is a Happy Time" came to be one of the all-time hits in our early childhood home. At the hint of selfishness, Gail would spring into song, clapping her hands, singing with enthusiasm,

> A sharing time is a happy time,
> > a happy time, a happy time.
> We share our books, and we share our toys,
> And that's a happy time.

I did not have to consult my notes to remember the words to this song. Nor would our children. They are so burned into the soil of our souls from sheer repetition by someone we love. All of us in this family might sheepishly confess that we hear the song, playing somewhere in our souls, even in our adulthood on those occasions when the question arises: Shall I be generous in the matter that faces me right now?

It seems reasonable to suggest that the majority of character-forming convictions are likely to have been set in place in the human experience in the first five years. And the mother, the father, and other family members are the growers.

Matthew Arnold in his poem "Rugby Chapel" pays supreme honor to his father. At one point he says of him:

> If, in the paths of the world,
> Stones might have wounded thy feet,
> Toil or dejection have tried
> Thy spirit, of that we saw
> Nothing—to us thou wast still
> Cheerful, and helpful, and firm!

What a child sees and hears in those significant lives goes on to be the first formation of convictions and character patterns at the base of his or her experience. No wonder Jesus warned such potentially significant people: handle the soul of a child poorly and it will be better for you if a millstone was hung about your neck and you were dropped into the sea. Obviously, Jesus felt rather strongly about this development of convictions in a child's life.

I must dare to speculate with this question: Do we inherit convictions? Is there the chance that some convictions and character traits are passed on to us through inheritance? Are some things written on the DNA codes that form us? My own personal answer is yes, that we carry with us the memories and some of the traits of the "fathers and mothers" who have gone before us. Their pain, their griefs, their noble instincts, and their dreams. Perhaps they become part of the sources that form us. They can be family sources we would want to embrace because they convey great strength to us. Or they can be sources we would want to renounce because they cast a destructive influence over us.

*A second source of convictions comes from the stories we hear.* From them we absorb the traits and characteristics of our heroes. Among the great storytellers in my earliest years was a single woman, Elizabeth McCall, with whom I spent precious time on summer vacations. It is almost fifty years since I bounded down the hill each morning to her summer cabin with the anticipation of hearing one more biographical story of a great pioneer missionary, often a martyr. There were other stories told by Miss McCall. She had a massive repertoire of stories of children from all over the world. How they handled their little fictional dramas did much to prepare me for the dramas that were coming my way. Convictions were growing as the seeds of the stories fell deep into my soul.

There were the vacation Bible school and Sunday school stories visualized not on video screen but on the flannelgraph. Week after week we saw the same paper characters put on the flannelgraph, but each time they were given different names and placed in different contexts. And our imaginations adjusted to the situation. We learned the stories of the biblical greats: Moses, David, Esther, Hannah, Jonah, Peter, John, and Paul. Wonderful stories! Told over and over again until they seeped like overflowing water into the nooks and crannies of our souls and grew there like mushrooms, harvested later as convictions and character.

The books: they were a source of convictions. In my childhood it was Bernard Palmer's *Sugar Creek Gang Series,* a set of books that told the stories of boys my age and their experiences in one adventure after another. There were the tough boys, the softhearted ones, the older, and the younger. And each added to my depository of extended views of the world and how one might act in similar circumstances. Convictions were growing in the reading of those books.

As one ages, *it becomes possible to learn convictions through abstract principles.* These are usually insights of learning that happen in the process of a disruptive moment. In a moment as a prep school athlete, a coach writes a letter whose premise is this: "If you quit in a tough moment like this, you'll likely set in motion a pattern of quitting throughout the rest of your life when other moments are difficult." Somehow the principle gets through the resistance filters and lodges in the soil of the soul. It becomes a conviction to be drawn upon time after time when times get tough, and one hears an inner voice saying, "I saw it through then, and I can see this through now."

There is another day when a seminary professor takes note of the fact that I have cut several of his classes to meet a deadline on another presentation. And of this presentation he says, "It was a good presentation but not a great one. Because you sacrificed your routine obligations to pursue something else." Once again a principle enters deep within and grows. It becomes a way of life: stay faithful to the routines.

*Then there are of course those principles that become convictions because they emerge from the Christian's ultimate source literature: the Bible.* This is why new Christ-followers are urged to go to the Bible on a daily basis. Remember the mission of Ezra: "For Ezra had prepared his heart to seek the Law of the LORD, and to do it, and to teach statutes and ordinances in Israel" (Ezra 7:10).

Here the Bible itself becomes the teacher. St. Paul writes, "We have received, not the spirit of the world, but the Spirit who is from God, that we might know the things that have been freely given to us by God" (1 Cor. 2:12). He is telling us that when a curious person comes to the Scripture, a supernatural event is capable of happening. Truth that is bigger than words is likely to fly off the page and head straight for the soul where like a seed it begins to grow into a conviction:

> For the word of God is living and powerful, and sharper than any two-edged sword, piercing even to the division of soul and spirit, and of joints and marrow, and is a discerner of the thoughts and intents of the heart (Heb. 4:12).

This Bible is no impotent piece of literature. Its truths seek the soul—like filings seek a magnet—in order to begin the process of forming convictions. The Bible presses us to learn that love must displace hate and anger; that forgiveness is more powerful than retribution; that generosity is greater than greed; that peacemaking is more effective than saber rattling; and that humility is more noble than arrogance and pride. These are not natural exchanges: they must be formed as convictions that then will give birth to character.

*I think it worthwhile to mention that sometimes convictions are the result of life in a community of spiritually minded people who have a convenant to live in a certain way for the mutual benefit of everyone.*

St. Paul has this in mind, for example, when he challenges us to think of the "weaker brother" (1 Cor. 8:11). His point is obvious: it is a good thing to ask how your behavior or your attitude is going to affect others. And if it is going to demoralize them or lead them toward sin because they do not share your level of maturity, then you may have to be diligent to set rights aside and choose to do what is good for the community.

A parent does this for his or her children. We chose to form a conviction about having alcoholic beverages in our home. We saw no sense in exercising a freedom when it could become the gateway to the problem of alcohol in the lives of our son and daughter. We forged convictions about excessive acquisition of material things because we desired that our children learn discipline in their spending habits. There were occasions when our choices to act or not to act were purely built upon what was best for our children or others watching from a distance.

*We must not overlook the possibility that convictions are also formed out of the consequences of failure.* When a person has failed—so terribly failed that the results burn the soul with a heat beyond imagination—one of two things is possible. The first possibility is a bitter spirit that learns nothing and perhaps, in its darkened condition, even lays the tracks toward continuing failure.

The alternative is better by far. Fail and hurt so badly as a result that a horror of any form of repetition becomes a conviction in itself. The fear of such sin and the personal reminder of its consequences become so prominent, the soul says "never again." And in the process a conviction is fully formed, stronger than ever.

"The sins of some men are obvious," St. Paul wrote, "reaching the place of judgment ahead of them; the sins of others trail behind them" (1 Tim. 5:24 NIV). Some of us have failures on our records that are known to anyone who is curious. We have tasted public humiliation, which at the time seemed worse than death.

Others who have failed somewhere along the line may have been fortunate that what happened in their lives never saw the light of day, and they were able to deal with the consequences on a private basis. The most important thing, however public or private our personal sadness, is whether we have forced the failure to become a teacher of character for the future. Questions like these drive the teaching.

- What does your failure mean?

- What weakness does it reveal in your nature?

- What must be done to recompense this failure?

- What conviction will you form to prevent this failure from happening again?

- And how will you use the lessons of this failure to be of value to you and others in the future?

These human propensities to failure often undermine the great structures and neutralize the great skills that humanity works so hard to develop. Harry Emerson Fosdick, well-known preacher of an earlier era, frequently alluded to the Great Wall of China, erected by mass labor and heavy governmental expense. This wall seemed at the time to be the guarantee the Chinese were seeking that they would be safe from all invaders. But it didn't work. Not because it was inadequate as a physical barrier. But because guards along the wall were open to bribes. On one occasion Fosdick said, "It was the human element that failed. What collapsed was character which proved insufficient to make the great structure men had fashioned really work."

There is one thing worse than a failure, and that is the failure to learn from the failure and turn it into a positive strength. The soul longs to learn. This is the great strength of Simon Peter: that his failures became the foundation of his later greatness as a holy apostle.

Remember this man whose courage failed on the night when he'd promised to stand side by side with his Lord. This man who in this moment of "spiritual experience" had promised his energy and his blood. But who reneged on the promise at the first hint of danger.

The beauty of this man was that he learned from his failure. And we have him around today as apostle, father of the church, and Epistle writer because Jesus went back, dusted him off, and gave him a fresh start.

Is Peter thinking of these failure moments when he writes these verses?

> Giving all diligence, add to your faith virtue, to virtue knowledge, to knowledge self-control, to self-control perseverance, to perseverance godliness, to godliness brotherly kindness, and to brotherly kindness love. For if these things are yours and abound, you will be neither barren nor unfruitful in the knowledge of our Lord Jesus Christ. *For he who lacks these things is shortsighted, even to blindness, and has forgotten that he was cleansed from his old sins* (2 Pet. 1:5–9, emphasis mine).

The pearls that so many people prize as precious jewelry were once formed in the shell of an oyster in the sea. It is said that each pearl is the product of sand that has gotten in the shell and has become an irritant. This is the possibility that comes with the difficult moments in which one has given in to temptation and violated the laws of God. Because of God's restorative space, a pearl of great conviction is likely to form about failure, and the loss of a battle becomes the prelude to winning a great personal war.

Finally, *convictions are developed on the basis of regular self-examination.* That was the point of the psalmist:

> Search me, O God, and know my heart;
> Try me. . . .
> And see if there is any wicked way in me,
> And lead me in the way everlasting (Ps. 139:23–24).

In the world of business, companies follow this principle with their employees. A man in our congregation is vice president of sales for a major hotel chain in our region. I met him the other day in the lobby of one of his competitors.

"What in the world are you doing here?" I said with mock shock. "Does your boss know that you're in a place like this?" Perhaps I was covering up my dis-ease at being discovered there myself.

He grinned, looked over his shoulder as if to make sure no one heard him, and said, "I'm in places like this all the time. I like to see what the competition is doing. Keeps us on our toes. And we learn from them."

We sat down in the lobby, and the conversation about learning experiences continued. He told me something I'd never known.

"We actually have a contract with a company that sends people into our hotels all the time. They check in as guests or come to our restaurants. And then they provoke situations that give them a chance to see 'how our employees will handle things. For example, they'll tell the desk clerk that they're locked out of their room. Or they'll complain that a meal is poorly cooked. Or they'll make a request that their laundry be expedited. Lots of things like that. Then we get reports about how our people have handled them."

"There's got to be a story here that I can use in a sermon," was my response.

And there was. The psalmist was asking God to do the same thing this company was going to do for my friend's hotel. My version of what was on the psalmist's mind:

Check out my soul and tell me what You see, O God. Test me!
Play back to me what You discern of my convictions so that when

the heat in life is turned up, I'll have confidence in the possibility of a God-pleasing attainment.

Such self-examination on a regular basis—when done under the influence of the Bible and God's presence—yields positive results.

## Can Character Be Rebuilt?

But what happens when the self- or soul-examination points up deficiency of character? *Can disappointing character patterns be rebuilt?* This is no small question.

Answer: emphatically yes! St. Paul's character was rebuilt; Simon Peter's was; and so was Jonah's. And so can yours and mine.

We rebuild it by forming new personal vows and covenants. And we hammer them into our souls just as a carpenter pounds a spike into a hard piece of wood. One swat at a time.

Benjamin Franklin believed in this process. He developed a list of thirteen "virtues" that he wanted to nail into the depths of his life. He carried a copy of his vows and covenants with him during all the years of his adult life. It is said that he evaluated himself on a daily basis, the criteria being this "list of virtues." He went further. Each week he pushed himself to treat one of the virtues with particular seriousness. "I always carried my little book with me," he writes,

> and it may be well my posterity should be informed that to this little artifice, with the blessing of God, their ancestor owes the constant felicity of his life down to his seventy-ninth year, in which this is written.

And what were some of those virtues? Here are some samples:

SILENCE: Speak not but what may benefit others or yourself; avoid trifling conversation.

FRUGALITY: Make no expense but to do good to others or yourself; that is, waste nothing.

SINCERITY: Use not hurtful deceit; think innocently and justly; speak accordingly.

HUMILITY: Imitate Jesus and Socrates.

One gains the impression that Franklin was quite aware that a tide of substandard behavior would flow from an untidy soul if he did not give daily attention to positive convictions that would frame a higher level of behavior and attitude. These four and the other nine I've not listed point to a key reason why Franklin was so forceful as a leader in the formation of the American nation.

The front pages of my journal include similar pages. My "operating convictions," as I call them, have been in the making for several years since I was compelled to a strenuous reappraisal of my entire structure of character. They were slowly formed as I made a deliberate attempt to rebuild my character in the company of Christ.

I'm afraid I wasn't as economic as Franklin and his list of virtues. I decided, for example, to list two sets of convictions: one set in the form of goals and objectives, and the other set in the form of principles that spoke to those dimensions of my life where I sensed God (the divine hotel inspector) poking and prodding at me for greater maturity.

## Goals and Objectives

In regard to goals and objectives, I found seven areas where I believed Jesus was calling me to think through where He was wanting to lead me.

1. My physical life: how I take care of my body
2. My relational life: how I deal with my marriage, my family, my friends
3. My intellectual life: how I take care of my mind
4. My vocational life: how, where, and why I do my job
5. My financial life: how I manage my money
6. My recreational life: how I rest, manage pleasure
7. My spiritual disciplines: how I commune with God

It seemed good to me to acknowledge the separate pursuits of each of these areas. What did I want to do with each of them? Either I would bring my life and resources into *a design* that was pleasing to God, or I would find my life being lived *by default*—by the pressure and influences of those around me. And St. Paul warned of the latter in words so famously translated by J. B. Phillips: *Don't let the world squeeze you into its mold!*

And so, as I felt impulsed by God's inner voice, I wrote into my journal some of my beliefs or convictions about these areas. I covenanted with myself and God that I would regularly consult these statements and measure my life-growth against them.

In the physical dimensions of my life, I wrote,

My objective is to keep my body in good health through positive habits, exercise, nutrition, and weight discipline.

In the area of the relational, I wrote,

My objective is to pursue loving solidarity with my wife in the pattern of Christ's love, to enjoy her friendship, and to make sure that her quality of life is the best I can make it. It is to be as faithful a family man as possible to my children and grandchildren. And, finally, it is to be a covenantal friend to a small circle of men and women to whom I'm drawn in community. Beyond that I want to be a contributing member to my generation, giving more to people than I take from them, investing energy in the development of the younger generation. I wish to be a man possessing "luminous personhood."

When it comes to my view of my intellectual life, I said in my journal,

My objective is to accelerate my learning curve whenever possible through reading and exposure to the thinking people of the day. To ask questions. To follow the advice of Fénelon who said, "If the truth be mighty, and God all-powerful, His children need not fear that disaster will follow freedom of thought."

In the area of the spiritual, my journal reads,

My objective is to be a focused, holy, obedient, and reverential man before God and His world. I seek to discipline my life so that it is controlled by the Spirit and so people are drawn one step closer to Christ because of me. And I am committed to pursuing the wholeness of my person: that the inner and the outer man may be one: no fragmentation, no inner dissonance, no repression of the truth, or difficult questions, or struggles.

Like Franklin, the great English lexicographer Samuel Johnson was committed to these sorts of exercises that had attracted me. You'll find this entry in his journal if you read very far into it:

I hope to cast my time into some stated method.
To let no hour pass by unemployed.
To rise by degrees more early in the morning.
To keep a journal.
I hope to read the whole Bible once a year as long as I live.

## Principles of Christlikeness

The second set of operating convictions emerged in terms of principles of, what were for me, Christlike behavior. Simple and positive statements focused on areas where I perceive that I struggle and where I need to grow. Also they are statements about what I believe following Jesus means in my personal world.

Some of the operating principles read like this:

- I will accept the truth that I am ultimately powerless to manage my life and that I am at my best when I surrender to heavenly power and purpose.

- I will try to maximize quiet for my spirit and think-time for my mind so that I am not taking my cues from the world around me but rather living inwardly, out of the soul. I will accept nothing short of being a self-possessed (which to me means Christ-possessed) person, my choices guided by my mission and objectives. It also means saying strategic no's and bringing the addiction to busyness under soul-management. "How rare it is to find a soul quiet enough to hear God speak." (Fénelon)

- I will derive my sense of personal value from the heavenly Father and not from the praise of people, the possession of things, or the accumulation of achievements. I will deal ruthlessly with self-deceit and unearned applause. My "scoreboard" is in heaven. I will follow the counsel of Thomas à Kempis: "If thou walk inwardly, thou shalt not weigh flying words. . . . Let not thy peace be in the mouths of men."

- I will repudiate that devilish "instinct" to slander or devalue others; I will either speak well of another or say nothing at all; I will use a vocabulary that is positive, seminal, and lovingly candid. And I will generate enthusiasm from within and spread it to others.

• I will be orderly in my private life and be dependable (a person of my word) in my relationship to others. I will think quality in each thing I do. I will persevere: not give up or quit easily.

• I will have a generous spirit; I will remain debt-free; I will maintain modesty in lifestyle; I will be sensitive to the poor. And I will not be fearful of the status of what the fathers called "littleness, hiddenness, and powerlessness."

Hidden throughout these and other statements that are too personal for me to share are phrases in quotes. They generally refer to reading I have done in the spiritual masters and where their words have become conviction-formers for me.

These are the sources from which character is formed: from the inheritance of our fathers, from the stories, from the actions of significant people in our worlds, from the Bible, from our failures, from our sense of guidance—that Jesus desires for us to be a more noble people, expressions of Christlikeness in character. And character grows out of the seedbed of convictions.

A few months before I wrote this chapter I was introduced to a man known to many in this country. His name: Ralph Showers. We were co-speakers at a conference for pastors.

When I first shook hands with him, I was instantly aware that he had a serious physical disability. Both of his arms were missing, and in the place of his hand, I found myself reaching out to shake a stainless steel prosthesis, an artificial hand.

As I came to know Ralph Showers in the following hours, I learned that this man in his late fifties was the director of Rainbow Acres in Arizona, a home and school for children and young people who were seriously retarded and mentally disabled. His stories of their work with the boys and girls at Rainbow Acres were simply amazing.

After I'd given two of my talks at the conference, I met Showers for breakfast the next day. I asked him to speak more about the kind of people who were at Rainbow Acres. Why, I was curious to know, had he contented himself to work with mentally disabled people all of his life? His reply set me back; it humbled me.

"I'm a simple man, Gordon, so simple that when I listened to you speak last night, I struggled to understand what you were saying."

Now that he had all of my attention, he went on: "You see, I'm mildly retarded myself. Every day is a frightening chore for me when I'm off traveling like this. I'm alone, and I can often become confused about what is going to happen next. But God has called me to this work with mentally disabled people, and as long as He gives me the strength, I'm going to do it. I think you'd find the boys and girls at Rainbow Acres an inspiration. Their ability to love one another far exceeds anything that you've seen in the rest of the world."

The discussion went on from there concerning how Rainbow Acres had first been started and paid for. It was then that Ralph Showers told me the story of the loss of his arms. He had been working on some of the early construction of the ranch and his arms accidentally touched a power line. They were instantly burned so badly that they had to be amputated.

But the story did not stop there.

Some time later four New York lawyers came to Arizona to work on a settlement between Ralph Showers and the company that owned the power line. They told Ralph's attorney that they would give Ralph a check for $325,000 that day if he would sign away all other claims concerning the accident. Ralph instantly agreed to the offer. And his attorney immediately protested. He told Ralph, "If you hold out and threaten a suit, they'll offer much more, as much as $1 million."

But Ralph said, "I'm not that kind of man. Besides the $325,000 is all I need to get Rainbow Acres up and started. Tell them I'll take their check."

A couple of years later Ralph Showers received a long-distance phone call. The caller identified himself and said, "I'm one of the attorneys who came from New York to make an offer to settle with you on your accident a couple of years ago. I want to tell you something."

Ralph invited him to go on.

The lawyer said, "When you accepted our offer of $325,000, the four of us who'd come to Arizona laughed. And we laughed all the way to the airport. We'd come authorized to pay you as much as $1 million. But you never asked for more, and we went home delighted with how much money we'd saved our client.

"But as time went on, I became bothered by what we'd done. We'd taken advantage of your good nature and your unwillingness to be adversarial. I don't think I've ever met someone like you. And learning something of your faith, I was driven to do some thinking. I ended up visiting with a Christian pastor back here in New York, and I want you to know that today I'm a Christian and a member of a church because of the kind of man you showed yourself to be."

That's character, and the convictions that formed it did not come instantly. They were formed through a lifetime of experience, of pain, of walking near Christ. That's heavy, heavy weight below the waterline.

Now when I think of the five-mile tunnel in Texas that was meant to help discover the secrets of the universe and now may be used to grow nothing but mushrooms, I get beyond the waste of government money as quickly as possible. And I go on to think of those ideal places where only special things can grow. Like the soul where convictions are formed. And when rightly formed, they produce a human being with noble character—someone who looks and acts like Christ. That's the kind of life God blesses.

# I CALL IT SOUL-TALK

*Wouldst thou pray in his temple?*
*Then pray within thyself; for thou*
*thyself are the true temple of the*
*living God.*
*—Augustine*

A COUPLE OF years ago I spent ten days solo-hiking in the Swiss
Alps. Other than negotiating the price of sleeping space in the
Alpine mountain hut or saying an occasional "I-greet-you-in-the-
name-of-God" to a passing walker, I don't think I engaged in any
other conversations for the entire time. For an introvert like me,
this—aloneness and Switzerland—seems close to what heaven
must be like.

The spiritual masters might liken my experience to a retreat of
stillness. Then, too, some of them just might have frowned when
they learned that I enjoyed myself so much.

Ten days of virtual aloneness amount to no small learning
experience. Enveloped in enforced quietness, one is likely to move
in the below-the-waterline direction of the soul rather than the
direction of the many noise-centers that sit about the periphery of
life. On Alpine paths there are no portable stereos, no cellular
phones, no persuasion messages from signs, and no million-and-
one people clawing for attention. Apart from beautiful views, there
is nothing more than what one can find in the inner person.

This intense experience of going inward can be a surprising and an unnerving one, and frankly, I was not prepared for it. If someone had ever told me what could happen in such aloneness, I'd not heard the message.

I made two discoveries during this inward journey toward my soul. First, I found how natural it could be—as a Christ-follower—to worship. Once the conscious part of myself came to grips that there was not going to be external distraction, it began to see things in a new light. I found it relatively easy to look at cloud formations, wildflowers in mountain meadows, and majestic snowcapped vistas and cry out to God with thanksgiving for such remarkable glory. Sounds like the large, mellow bells that hung around Swiss brown cows were like a choir whose corporate song is unvarnished praise. Smells like newly cut grass from a farmer's sickle seemed so clean and symbolic of the freshness of a "mercied" heart. The sound of water crashing down a slab of vertical rock seemed a reminder of heavenly power and strength.

The aloneness also encouraged a bevy of recollections. Of friends for whom I am very grateful. Of a family who bring me continual joy. Of the opportunities to preach the Bible and encourage the development of people in Christlikeness. "It doesn't get any better than this," I heard myself say as I counted my unmerited blessings and reviewed my life.

And so my walk in aloneness became a seedbed for thoughts like these. In my stillness I found everything to be a cause for praise and worship of the Creator whose glory is reflected in all of this. I actually remember saying to myself after one such nonstop period of worship, "Maybe I've finally had a personal revival. All I seem to want to do is worship." People who had seen me from a distance might have been excused if they concluded that I was a bit crazy. For I would occasionally stop my walk, kneel in the grass, and lift my arms toward heaven and speak aloud to the Father in exaltation. Who could have understood such antics if they had not wiretapped my soul?

Unfortunately, that's not the whole story. For my aloneness paved the way for a second set of thoughts. Remember, I said there were two discoveries, and the second was less than noble.

My inclination toward inwardness not only stimulated worship and praise, but it also caused me to rediscover personal darkness. There was the hard part. In the isolation I found that my mind could easily jump from rapturous praise to the most embarrassing, subpar thoughts. Events, mostly negative ones, covering almost fifty years of life began to crowd through my mind like a parade. Memories of old angers and resentments, issues I thought had long been settled, sadnesses, and regrets. From nowhere came self-accusations and base ambitions that had no business being in the soul of one who thought he'd long since encountered Christ at the cross.

One can talk about transparency, vulnerability, honesty, loving self-disclosure all one wants, but some of this stuff from the dark and depth of the soul was not the sort I'd want anyone to know about. What emerged was enough to cause one to drop to the grass—not to worship but to repent—and repeat the words of St. Paul, which I've already noted elsewhere, "O wretched man that I am! Who will deliver me from this body of death?"

So you can picture my increasing consternation. I felt like I was standing on a mental and spiritual continental divide. Turn to the left, and I was exulting the living God and His glory with something near ecstasy. Turn to the right, and I was groveling in a cesspool of thought patterns that were terrible to behold.

My Swiss hike taught me something of how deep—how infinitely deep—is this soul below the waterline, how much capacity there is in every one of us to lean toward righteousness *or* evil, and how important it is to consult the soul while we live in a world that wishes to assert that the soul doesn't exist or is simply not important. As one father of the faith said, "Salute thyself and see what thy soul doth wear."

I came to realize that the Swiss hike was as close to prolonged prayer as I may ever experience in this part of my eternal life. There I came in touch with something so profound that I can only call it authentic prayer in order to set it off from the kind of ordinary, so-often-meaningless prayer I hear coming from myself when I'm going through the motions.

I think that what happened there in the upper meadows and the mountain passes is what happens when people begin to seriously pray. The light of God's glory becomes vividly bright, and the darkness of the uncleansed soul becomes remarkably dark.

And therein lies a problem I've had. Most of my prayers, the inauthentic kind, have not had either the intensity or the duration that would stimulate the sort of soul-revealing experience I had in Switzerland.

I've been bothered by this, and I've tried hard to do something about it. I am only marginally successful, tempted sometimes to discouragement, but glad that there is a prompting within me to keep on pursuing. And I'll not stop!

Authentic prayer of any kind is the talk of the soul. When one truly prays, one—to use psalm-language—lifts up the soul. When I talk to a friend, however, I may talk on various other levels. A mindless cliché can sometimes do the job (How are you? Terrific! End of talk). I can talk out my feelings when I'm miffed or overjoyed (I'm down; I'm sad; I'm elated). I hope that I talk mostly from my mind and offer opinions and judgments that are beneficial (Have you thought about this? Let me make this observation).

I'm sorry to say, however, that I don't think I—or most anyone else—talk much (or enough) out of the soul. And that's something I'm trying to work on.

Genuine prayer means talking out of the soul to God. And I'll venture the opinion that *genuine fellowship* (biblical koinonia) means talking out of the soul to another as we join in the process of prayer. And who of us has known that many experiences of authentic communication on this level? Perhaps just occasionally? "If two or three of you agree together," Jesus says. Perhaps the agreement of which He speaks is that soul-level connection we experience as we pray together about matters of mutual concern.

It was Samuel Chadwick, I believe, who once suggested that Satan fears nothing more than a saint on his or her knees before God. He's got to be right about that if one takes the measure of the biblical personalities and is reminded that almost everything of kingdom significance that they did followed the exercise of serious prayer.

What Christ-follower of evangelical persuasion does not agree with that and talk about it? And that is more than part of the problem. We are part of a community that talks a lot about prayer but does relatively little of it. Little soul-talk. And we do what I'm trying to avoid doing in this writing: preach to each other about how important prayer is and why we should be doing it. And then go off and do something else feeling that just by talking about prayer and its importance, we've relieved ourselves of the responsibility of being prayerful people.

The Swiss Alps experience is not the only time I've been mystified by the strange talk of the soul. Like others, I've had these unusual moments when prayer seemed so natural to life, when it seemed the only sensible thing to do. Take, for example, the night in the middle of a Kansas blizzard when no one was going anywhere and our one-month-old son was burning up with a high fever. I held him toward heaven and begged God for the lowering of that fever. I poured out my soul in a passion that I am reluctant to describe. And God heard my prayer.

Or the days when I had to face the fact of my own personal sinfulness and lift a darkened heart to God asking for mercy. Again, the passion of tearful soul-talk. The no-holds-barred groaning of the inner being, which suddenly realizes personal sorrow that no other can share.

There were those unforgettable days when I faced a decision that seemed ten times larger than me. No human wisdom, no advice, no decision-making tree seemed to help. And exhausted of wit, I came to God asking for the insight that only heaven seems to offer. Those were times when I knew the edges of soul-talk.

But as I say, we speak much of these things. But are liable to resort to them more as the exception than the rule. Why? These additional thoughts.

*First, soul-talk, authentic prayer, almost never happens apart from silence and where there are minimal external distractions.* There are exceptions. Peter's cry "save me" on the Galilee waters was definitely soul-talk. But it certainly wasn't in a context of silence; rather, it was desperation (and that sometimes helps). Elijah seems to have stepped off to one side when amidst the crowd up on Mt. Carmel; his conversation with God seems very personal, very hush-hush. But maybe I'm wrong.

Nevertheless, silence is more the proper environment for soul-talk. And one could easily imagine that our modern culture has been guided in an evil sense to deny all of us the necessary silence to move toward the inner experience. Television, incessant musical backgrounds, and cellular phones are not inducements to silence. The visual chatter of our computers and faxes, the network of relationships we have all acquired that are much larger than the village-sized networks of our grandparents. If one succumbs to the seductions of noise, there will never be prayer that can be described as soul-talk. Mind-talk perhaps. Emotion-talk, maybe. But not soul-talk: the kind that energizes worship and sharpens one's view of the world while also exposing personal evil.

*Time is a second element.* One does not normally engage in soul-talk as one might in the shallow, glib conversations we often have with one another. I don't want to make soul-talk sound hard, but the fact is that a period of preparatory time may have to elapse before the soul is ready to engage in heavenly intimacy. I imagine the soul as something that hides from all the noise and busyness of life. Can I suggest that it has to be coaxed into action? And the coaxing may take time. Time that most of us do not think we have.

I don't think my soul really swung into significant motion in Switzerland for at least two or three days. Then when it got the message that I was really alone and quiet, it never seemed to want to stop speaking . . . from both the dark and the bright sides.

We have all been taught the importance of daily prayer. But I suspect that one would profit more from a weekly experience of three or four prayerful hours than just a few minutes each day. It's not a fair comparison, perhaps, but my intuition suggests that I'm "righter than wronger" about this.

*A third element has to do with deriving assistance from that body of saints I earlier called the spiritual masters.* Many of them wrote wonderful prayers and meditations as they engaged in soul-talk. Most of them had time we do not have, silence we've been denied, and the encouragement of a culture that expected some people to make soul-talk their vocation. Pastors, monks, hermits, for example. The *Confessions* of Augustine (an urban man) and the *Imitation* of Thomas à Kempis (kind of a rural man) are two samples. *The Book of Common Prayer*, the prayers of John Baillie (a more modern personality), the writings of A. W. Tozer, the insights of Faber, Fénelon, Teresa of Avila, and St. John of the Cross come to mind. Chambers's *Utmost*, Carmichael's challenges, and Wesley's hymns. These are all soul-talk in one way or another, and they pull and tug at the soul, provide it a language and thought forms with which to speak a quiet word to the Father. And how can one forget the Psalms as a source of great prayer?

Some of us were raised to avoid these sorts of writings, believe it or not. The superior way, we were told, was "to pray from the heart." But there come days when my heart (or my soul) feels empty; it simply has nothing to say. And like the priming of a pump, the words and insights of the spiritual masters are an aid to get things going. Just as the composer of a song offers me a melody and words to express joy, so the spiritual greats give us prayers to express what we may—for a moment—find inexpressible.

I have found the journaling I've mentioned frequently in this book to be a great assist to my soul-talk attempts. On those days when coldness has been more than a matter of outer New England temperatures, I have found myself unable to produce hardly a coherent word from soul-level. The journal has helped at such times. "Modern" that I am, I journal into my computer, and I have learned to write and describe to the Father in journal form my hardness of soul and spirit. Usually, after three or more paragraphs of frank talk, I find the inner stone begins to break up.

My journals are full of talk arising from the soul. Lists of things for which I'm thankful, hosts of things about which I'm embarrassed, a veritable catalog of hopes on behalf of my friends and congregation.

*A last pertinent element in soul-talk is patience*. Patience! The ability to wait. When I was younger, my impatience was (by comparison) troublesome. I would privately observe to my wife that I saw little one-for-one connection between my prayers and results. That was the conclusion of a small-thinker with too few years of life under his belt, one who could not see things over the long haul. Today is different. Fifty-plus years do not exactly provide a long view, but they are long enough to realize that what one says from the soul must be cast in the perspective of eternity, the promises and purposes of God. I am praying prayers that may not have their answer until long after I am in the grave. And that's OK. I now know that God has never been oblivious of one word I've spoken from the soul in His direction. The timing is His; the patience must be mine.

This Mysterious One to whom we direct our souls moves with agonizing slowness on some days and with lightning speed on others. One lays no demands, no time lines, and no measurements before Him. One bows, speaks the language of the soul, and then waits. And often does not tell others what he is waiting for. Conversation from soul to heaven is enough.

I am bothered by the thought that silence, time, touch with the spiritual ancients, self-disclosure in a journal, and patience are not commodities in great supply today. And if not, then prayer may take the form of shallow words, empty cliches, quick-burst comments, and religious soliloquies.

Give me soul-talk! Ten words of it spoken below the waterline of life are worth a thousand of the other kind. Soul-talk is what comes from the bottom of one's inner world. Where God is likely to dwell through union in Christ. Where one will make painful discoveries about self's propensities and improprieties and reach for grace. Where one will look at creation and its possibilities with fresh eyes and worship. Where one will come to understand that every minute spent in the divine Presence is worth much more than an ounce of gold.

# WHERE DOES THE ENERGY COME FROM?

*Deity indwelling men! That, I say, is
Christianity, and no man has
experienced rightly the power of
Christian belief until he has known
this for himself as a living reality.
Everything else is preliminary to this.*
—A. W. Tozer

EACH CHAPTER OF this book raises topics that can be compared
to beads of a necklace. They describe the characteristics and
actions of a life God might choose to bless. Beads can be things of
minute beauty. But one thing is necessary if beads are to be
collected and formed into something that can be hung about the
neck. The beads need a string.

The string that draws the beads of this book together is the
third member of the Trinity: *the Holy Spirit.*

We have been taught that the Holy Spirit is variously repre-
sented in Scripture with such pictures as breath, wind, comforter,
advocate, and companion. Words like these—metaphorical words
actually—are necessary because the Holy Spirit is not visible.
Only what the Spirit accomplishes in and through people is likely
to be visible. The words used to describe the Holy Spirit always
speak of the special presence and strength of God. They reveal to
us a notion of a divine energy that empowers a person to be and to
do something otherwise thought difficult or impossible. It is a
power that turns common people into exceptional citizens in the
kingdom of God.

If there is a life God blesses, you can be sure that the Holy Spirit is at the root. One sees evidences of what happens through the Bible when men and women were filled with the third member of the Trinity. Among the most famous is Gideon, God's chosen leader for the Israelites in a time when they were being overwhelmed by enemies who swept across their land.

On one particular occasion when thousands of the enemies made their periodic invasion, Scripture says—here the literal Hebrew rendering is helpful—"Then the Spirit of the Lord *clothed* Gideon." Soon after, he accomplished extraordinary things with a small band of soldiers under his command. The enemy's thousands were licked by Gideon's hundreds.

A walk through Christian biography will demonstrate that an extraordinary percentage of the men and women whose lives God blessed also speak of a special moment when they felt clothed by this same Holy Spirit. For some, it was a sudden event; for others, something slow, almost imperceptible. But the difference between life before and life after was the contrast between night and day.

The nineteenth-century evangelist D. L. Moody spoke of such a "clothing" experience in which his life below and above the waterline was irrevocably changed. At a time when he felt particularly inept and impotent in his soul, he found himself calling out to heaven for new spiritual depths and energies. God answered the call, and a moment came in which Moody was greatly touched by the Spirit of the Lord. He rarely spoke of that moment. But when he did, he was careful never to boast of what had happened. Clearly, he was deeply humbled that it had even happened:

> My heart was not in the work of begging . . . I could not appeal. I was crying all the time that God would fill me with his Spirit. Well, one day, in the city of New York—O, what a day!—I cannot describe it; it is almost too sacred an experience to

name. Paul had an experience of which he never spoke for fourteen years. *I can only say that God revealed himself to me, and I had such an experience of his love that I had to ask him to stay his hand.* I went to preaching again. The sermons were not different; I did not present new truths, and yet hundreds were converted. *I would not now be placed back where I was before that blessed experience if you should give me all the world*—it would be as small dust in the balance. (emphasis mine)

We must think about this! Is what happened to Gideon, to Moody, and to a myriad of others like them a unique experience, limited to just a few? Or was it something designed to touch all those who seek the hand of God?

I write about this matter of the Holy Spirit with great reluctance. It is too large and too sacred a subject to treat with triviality. I have a fear of conveying something too easily achievable like the spiritual experiences of which I wrote in an earlier chapter. And yet I have an even greater fear of neglecting the subject and rendering all other parts of this book as meaningless. For without the work of the Holy Spirit, alive and living within one's soul, all other activities and meditations are indeed worthless.

The Holy Spirit could be called the family Spirit of God. In biblical times the head of the house placed great emphasis upon handing on to the firstborn son not only the family fortune but also the family spirit. This was called the moment of "blessing." There was a powerful conviction that a family line had a spirit resident in it, and it was passed on from generation to generation. For a man, not to have a son to pass on the family spirit was catastrophic.

The family spirit conveyed the honor of the family. It carried a sense of the family's character, its mission. To be blessed with the family spirit was to have the voices of your father and your father's fathers in your soul. All of their wisdom, their power, and their experience was passed on to you when you received the family spirit.

This idea of the family spirit and its passage through blessing from generation to generation may explain some of the strange passages of the Older Testament in which an entire family was executed in judgment for one man's sins. The sin of Achan, for example, is treated with unusual harshness, it seems to us.

Why would it be necessary to execute not only Achan but his entire family, even his children? In a culture like ours where we perceive every human being as a "stand-alone" individual, we have no notion of such a mystical idea of family connectedness. And yet it was perceived that the spirit causing Achan to disobey God could be inherited by his children, and the spirit must be eradicated.

This idea of a family spirit is also why Abraham, our spiritual father, suffered so greatly when he and his wife, Sarah, passed through childbearing years and had no son to show for it. He found himself facing the reality that his family line would be extinct and that the family spirit would die with him. He had no son to whom he might give his blessing.

St. Paul understood this great concern of Abraham, and he writes much about it. He recalls the great Genesis story and tells how God came to Abraham and promised him not only a son but an enduring nation of sons. It would be a family line whose population would match the number of stars. No small family!

In the days of Abraham, the sperm of the man was not as much seen for its physiological potency as it was regarded as conveying the spirit of man. And a sterile man could be said to have a dead spirit. How kind of God, then, to give Abraham His Holy Spirit. And Paul, taking note of this great Older Testament miracle, says that all of us who have trusted in Christ receive that same Spirit. The Spirit first given to Abraham is given also to us through Jesus. All who follow after Jesus receive the Holy Spirit, the family Spirit of heaven.

There has been much confusion over the Holy Spirit down through the history of the Christian church, and unfortunately, that confusion is likely to go on throughout the ages to come. Good and godly people have taken positions of varying kinds to explain the role and work of the Holy Spirit. Sadly, those positions have sometimes become so hardened that ruptures in friendship and partnership have occurred as a result. This seems silly. For the Spirit was given by God to bring the family together. We were meant to continue the honor of the heavenly family, to be a credit to our heavenly Father. And all too often we are not. We are not a united family; we are a divided one.

Paul wrote of the ideal familyness God has in mind for us and how the Holy Spirit is given to make it all happen:

> You are all sons of God through faith in Christ Jesus, for all of you who were baptized into Christ have clothed yourselves with Christ. There is neither Jew nor Greek, slave nor free, male nor female, for you are all one in Christ Jesus. If you belong to Christ, then you are Abraham's seed, and heirs according to the promise (Gal. 3:26–29 NIV).

This, Paul was trying to teach his new congregations of Christ-followers, was the genius of Christian faith: that when a person, like Abraham, trusted or believed in God, a new spirit, the one we call the Holy Spirit, entered his life replacing the old, dead, impotent one that perished because of sin:

> The Spirit Himself bears witness with our spirit that we are children of God, and if children, then heirs—heirs of God and

joint heirs with Christ, if indeed we suffer with Him, that we may also be glorified together (Rom. 8:16–17).

If a person has made the choice to live out of the soul, Paul's message becomes very important. For we are being told that living out of the soul involves the presence of God's Spirit in the deepest places. Again, Paul: "The love of God has been poured out in our hearts [souls] by the Holy Spirit who was given to us" (Rom. 5:5).

All the things we have thought about through the pages of this book become living principles when they are strung together with this great truth: *that God Himself comes to dwell in the souls of people who open their lives to Him in faith*, just as did Abraham when God gave him the Spirit to replace his dead spirit.

To speak of the Holy Spirit is to speak of a divine Presence that enters the human experience. It was meant to be there in the very beginning—at creatión time. But the Presence was lost because the first man made a dreadful decision to "go it alone." What Jesus has come to offer is a redemptive process that brings us into line with the gift first received by Abraham. The Spirit, given to Abraham, is also given to us. And as it enters our souls through faith in Jesus, things of eternal significance are likely to happen. Like what?

When this Holy Spirit enters the soul below the waterline, at least three things seem to swing into motion.

*First, the Spirit begins to generate confidence that we are now part of God's family, His divine community.* An awakening of sorts happens, and one is aware of a new connection with both heaven and earth. One is part of the great church that God, St. Paul says, purchased with the blood of His Son, Jesus. One becomes alive with new affections, desires to worship, to serve, to pursue a quality of life that will be a pleasure to the giver of the Spirit, God

Himself. One desires to connect with people of like family characteristics and dreams.

It is great confidence that the Spirit generates within the
Christ-follower. The old fear that I do not belong anywhere is
squashed. The question of whether or not I am acceptable to God is
answered: I am because I am younger brother to Jesus, His Son.
The confidence that my soul shall live eternally in a fashion for
which it was created is enlarged. And I, in my ordinariness, inherit
a sense of destiny: I am a child in God's magnificent kingdom.

Responding to such confidence generated by the Spirit, Her-
bert Butterfield has written,

> Both in history and in life it is a phenomenon by no means rare
> to meet with comparatively unlettered people who seem to have
> struck profound spiritual depths . . . while there are many highly
> educated people of whom one feels that they are performing clever
> antics with their minds to cover a gaping hollowness that lies
> within.

## The Fruit of the Holy Spirit

*A second thing that begins to happen when we have this new
Spirit in us is that we begin to assume characteristics appropriate to
our new family connection.*

When I was a teenager, my parents (and a generous schol-
arship) made it possible for me to attend a fine prep school. The
upside of that experience was a great education. The downside:
except for summers, I was rarely able to go home to rejoin my
family.

Fortunately, I shared a room in the dormitory with a boy whose
home was not far from school, and his family welcomed me when-

ever I wished to join them. My roommate's parents were warm and loving people, and they were also more than generous.

When I would accompany my roommate to his home on many weekends, his father would meet us at the door. He would hand me a ten-dollar bill apparently knowing that I had little or no money with me. And as he would put it in my hand, he would say, "Gordon, when you are in our home, you're a member of the family, and you spend the family's money." Naturally, I was only too glad to assist the family in this spending as he so kindly suggested.

Because I loved going to that home, I paid careful attention to how one fit in. I could not be a real son to the father and the mother in that home, but I guess I desired to live out the role of a surrogate one. And one way to do that was to *act the real son.* So I watched my roommate carefully: how he treated his parents, how he responded to their requests, how he carried himself at the various functions. And I emulated him as much as was possible.

Thus, when I took note that my roommate wore a jacket and a tie to the dinner table, I was careful to wear them, too. And when I saw how high a premium was placed upon matters of social elegance and manners, I determined to please the parents as I saw the son pleasing them. I was careful to express appreciation, as he seemed to do; I would cause no trouble, and be courteous to guests who entered their home for a visit. These characteristics were the son's style; they would be mine.

My last name was different, but I acted as a member of the family emulating the family characteristics. And I did that by becoming like the son.

The Holy Spirit makes this possible when we choose to live out of the soul. There are definite living characteristics in the family of God. *Paul calls them the fruit of the Holy Spirit.* When the Spirit is given and takes residence within the soul of the Christ-follower, the evidence of that fact mounts in characteristics such as love, joy, peace, patience, kindness, goodness, faithfulness, gentleness, and self-control. They become the dominant traits of the family member. To the extent that they were not there before, change of life begins to happen.

I did not see my way of life at my roommate's home as a dutiful one. No one gave me a list of rules. I was simply so glad to be a part of a warm family after many days of living in a dormitory and eating institutional food that I was thrilled to fit in with my adopted family. I wished to please the ones who made me their guest, their "adopted son."

Living out of the soul is like this. The Spirit of God has entered the life of the Christ-follower. It is the same Spirit that God gave to Abraham and to Gideon. The same Spirit of Jesus, given to all who trust in Jesus as Savior, as Lord, as Elder Brother.

To be a member of *this family* is life's highest grace and privilege. To be invited into its fellowship is to be invited not just as a guest but as an adopted child. And that is where my simple story of school days breaks down. Ultimately, I was only a guest in my roommate's home. But in the family of God, I am adopted as a son. There on those weekends away from school I might role-play the position of a son, but I was only a guest. In God's family, there need be no role-playing. The Spirit has entered my soul; spiritual genetics have passed on the family temperament. And with it comes the passion to live out these Christ-honoring traits that Paul called the fruit of the Spirit.

## The Gifts of the Holy Spirit

The Spirit that God gave to Abraham and that comes to us through Jesus enlivens these characteristics of life, and the Spirit also offers certain capacities that Paul, Peter, and others referred to as "gifts." Capacities designed for the purposes of service: serving others in the world, serving God in worship.

When a son received the family spirit, there was also the sense that he received something of his father's skills. The spirit of the farmer; the spirit of the hunter; the spirit of the shepherd. My father's skills given to me: they are gifts he passes to me with his spirit.

God's Spirit comes to live in the soul of the Christ-follower. With that coming there is the implanting of new possibilities for service.

A world that knows little of the soul speaks only of skills and aptitude when it comes to extraordinary performance. It assumes that human beings possess certain natural talents and can acquire certain capacities. But the Christ-follower comes to understand these things differently. He or she comes to understand that there is an infusion of capacity that not infrequently carries an individual far beyond natural talent.

Think of Simon Peter, a simple fisherman, who, within three years of the time of meeting Jesus, stands in the center of Jerusalem and proclaims the gospel of Christ to a crowd numbering in the thousands. This is not merely a hidden talent suddenly springing to life; this is the Spirit within the soul of Peter making something happen that is at the initiative of heaven.

Years later Peter would speak of such giftedness, saying,

> Each one should use whatever gift he has received to serve others, faithfully administering God's grace in its various forms. If anyone speaks, he should do it as one speaking the very words of God. If anyone serves, he should do it with the strength God provides, so that in all things God may be praised (1 Pet. 4:10–11 NIV).

If the characteristics have something to do with being a member of the family, the gifts have something to do with serving the King of kings. Serving to His pleasure and with His approval in mind. These gifts are not for the development of a career, although more than a few have used them as such. They are rather for the building of the kingdom.

Some gifts empower others to grow, to elevate their lives from struggle. Other gifts proclaim the great "secrets" of God to those who have not known. Still other gifts are meant to provide discernment and insight to things otherwise not perceived. And finally, there are gifts that permit us to enlarge our capacity to worship the Lord. They lift us above our common language, even our physical limits. They give us the first hints of what a life centered in worship in eternity just may be like.


## The Power of the Holy Spirit

All of this is wrapped up in a word closely associated with the Holy Spirit throughout the Bible: the word *power*. One quickly gains a sense from the Bible that wherever the Holy Spirit is found in the lives of people, strange and wonderful things are likely to happen at any moment: young men prophesy; old men dream dreams. There are visions and possibilities; there are returns to wholeness and elevations to great accomplishment. There is discernment of hidden things, knowledge of mysteries. And there is capacity to love the unlovable and show grace and forgiveness to the worst of the worst. All this is part of the power of the Holy Spirit in the soul of a simple person.

*The Spirit offers a third possibility as He is pressed into the depths of our souls: empowerment.* "You shall receive power," Jesus tells His disciples. Why the need for power? Because humanity has lost so much of what it was designed to have.

The soul was meant to be a power station, a power base with virtually unlimited capacity in a magnificent creation. That power was moral, spiritual, creative, expressive, discerning, anticipating. But sin neutralized much of the power; humanity was left with a mere scintilla of what was supposed to be.

You often see hints of what that great power was meant to be like. The power of the artist to portray a rendition of a scene, a person, or even an idea. The power of the poet to use language to encapsulate a profound thought. The power of the composer; the power of the surgeon, the teacher, or the unusually effective leader in inspiring people.

Here and there we have hints of these amazing capacities that God meant for all of us to have. And this is meant to be one of the products of the indwelling Spirit of God that comes to replace the deadened part of our own spirits.

Life below the waterline is just that: *LIFE!* It is meant to be the energy center far below the waterline that provides the power to break through circumstances and situations bogging down the ordinary person.

When asked why God had anointed him to be the founder of a remarkable movement of spiritual force, St. Francis said,

This must be why the Lord has blessed my efforts. He looked down from heaven and must have said, "Where can I find the weakest, the smallest, the meanest man on the face of the earth?" Then he saw me and said, "Now I have found him. I will work through him, for he will not be proud of it nor take my honor away from myself. He will realize that I am using him because of his littleness and insignificance."

How sad when one engages with people in whom there is no such life. Where there is little more than existence, drawn like surface water, from places other than the soul.

Brigid Hermann has written,

> When we turn to the inner circle of the spiritual masters—the men and women, not necessarily gifted or distinguished, to whom God was a "living bright reality" which super naturalized through every day life and transmuted their homeliest actions into sublime worship—we find that their roots stuck deep into the soil of spiritual silence. Living in the world and rejoicing in human relationships, they yet kept a little cell in their hearts whither they might run to be alone with God.

It is a long time since Abraham groaned out his predicament to no one in particular: I have no son; my spirit within me is dead. And from out of the seeming darkness came a voice: I am with you. And you shall have a son and tons of sons. And God gave Abraham a new spirit. And He has given us this same Spirit if only we ask and then prepare our souls as fit dwelling places for this One who comes to live in us.

My wife, Gail, and I recently spent four years of our lives in New York City where we thoroughly enjoyed serving a congregation of young professional people. Every day was something of an adventure. When we left the city to return to Lexington, Massachusetts, we left a piece of our hearts behind. As we said good-bye to the people of Trinity Baptist Church, they presented us with a magnificent book of memories. Every page was made up of letters and pictures that would remind us in years to come of the ways in which we'd been involved in the lives of so many people.

There was the picture of the man who works for the New York

State prison system and does his best to bring Christ's presence into a cell block of hardened criminals. The young woman who is a social worker and gives all of her hours to people with AIDS who are dying with almost no contact from families who have abandoned them. The young actress who has been starring in one of Broadway's top musicals. The man who flies about the world representing one of the best consulting companies in America. The English couple who deal in porcelain antiques. The woman who works as a nurse on a night shift and then arrives at the church each Sunday morning with food for several hundred people at coffee hour. In the book are the memories of doctors, investment bankers, translators at the United Nations, and clothing designers. All of them and many others make up that congregation.

We had seen the Holy Spirit touch those lives, one after another. Not because we were there necessarily, but because the Spirit of Jesus was at the center of the congregational life itself. The city, like the disruptive moments on a stormy ocean, forced us all to grow . . . or drown in our souls. And we preferred growth. And grow we all did together.

Among these people I've mentioned, there is one who typifies all the rest. She has a prominent place in our memory book. Janet is an African-American woman who, five years ago, held an executive position in one of New York's top banks. We watched as her life was changed as the Spirit of Christ established residency in her soul. We saw a tough but gracious spirituality develop over a period of time that was awesome to behold.

When we first met Janet, we were impressed with her energy and her sharp mind. From the earliest moments there was also an unbridled reverence for Christ, a desire to grow in His likeness. That perspective always opens the door to great possibilities for becoming a life God blesses.

But there was also at least one powerful obstacle to Janet's development in Christlikeness. We came to realize that there were, hidden deep in her soul, some bottomless pits of anger. Two or three times each year, the anger would erupt followed by depression, and for a couple of weeks, Janet became incommunicative with even her closest friends. In such moments she could accept no love; she could give none. She simply withdrew from everything, and each time our anxiety for Janet grew greater.

As Janet became more committed to developing weight below the waterline of her life, she came to a disruptive moment where these periodic bursts of anger had to be dealt with. Either she was going to master the anger, or it was going to do irreparable damage to her.

I'm not sure that any one moment can be identified as the turning point, but if I had my vote, it would be for one Sunday morning when a dozen or more of us met for an hour of intercessory prayer. We sat, circled together in a small room on the second floor of the church building. As we prepared to pray, Janet suddenly spoke.

As best as I can remember her words, Janet said something like this: "I need your prayers today. I can feel anger beginning to grow within me. And if it happens, I'd like to suggest that you leave me alone. There's nothing you can tell me that will make it go away. And you'll probably just make me angrier if you try. So pray for me that this won't happen. And if it does, pray for me that God will heal me as quickly as possible. I don't like this anger any more than you do; it embarrasses me, and I'd give anything to get rid of it. I wish I knew where it's coming from."

We began to pray. And many of us prayed that morning for Janet. We asked the Holy Spirit to deliver her, to protect her, to heal her. There were tears triggered by our love for her, our sense of urgency over her struggle, and our desire to see this issue beaten in her life for the sake of Jesus.

When the prayer time was over, I asked Janet if we could talk privately for a moment. Since she wasn't angry yet, I wasn't worried that I was violating her earlier advice to stay away. "Janet," I said, "I have a thought for you. It may make no sense at all, but I want you to think about this." She nodded.

"I'm wondering if the anger you're feeling isn't coming from a source that's much deeper in you than you realize. What about the possibility that you're dealing with anger that comes from your mother's mother's mother? You and I have ancestors who came to this country under different circumstances. Yours probably did not come willingly. And I can only imagine what your great-great-grandparents must have gone through when they were brought here. Maybe the anger really belongs to them and speaks to how they were treated. Maybe it's been passed down to you in the family line, and you're feeling what they felt.

"If I'm right," I went on, "then you've got to concentrate on the event of forgiveness. Let a lot of grace clean out these pockets of anger."

Janet wept a bit and promised to think about what I'd said, and we went our separate ways. I'm not sure I know exactly what happened, but I know that Janet seemed to begin gaining measured victory over her anger from that time forward. The power of her anger began to dissipate. And though there were tough moments, she became an overcomer in this area of her life.

But that's not all. Janet went on to resign her job at the bank so that she could form a nonprofit organization focusing on young people in the inner city. Before long Janet was in and out of New York public schools talking to teenagers, convincing them not to give up the hopes of reaching their dreams. From her long hours with adolescents came Vehicles, a creative and very effective organizational effort at teaching young people and men and women of all ages how to pick and develop fulfilling careers and become responsible citizens.

I tell Janet's story at the end of this book because she reminds me of Michael Plant with whom I began this book. Like Plant, she was an expert at what she did. And like him, she faced some very tough storms in life. And also like Plant, she capsized. But unlike Michael Plant, she had enough weight below the waterline to be able to come about and begin sailing again. He went under; she didn't.

When I think of Janet Barrett, I am reminded of a woman who understood that what was below the waterline counted a lot more than what was above it. She'd heard the call of God to give back what she'd received.

Then again, she moved forward in life led by a vision. There was a mission; there were convictions; and there was a willingness to do the necessary soul-work that looked down and deep for the impurities that, untended, could become terrible obstacles. And soul-talk? I have known few people who came to reverence the power of prayer more than our friend Janet.

But aside from all of this, Janet's secret has been the fullness of the Spirit of Jesus in her. No sudden miracles that have made life become instantly easier. Just a daily opening of the heart and life to the entrance and residency of the Holy Spirit. A dependency on Him for protection, for wisdom, and for resources. And that perspective of deep humility has made all the difference.

Michael Plant's body was never recovered. Today, Janet Barrett puts in a full day in Harlem. You can find her almost anytime you head there. She's the one who has a life God blesses.

# THE LIFE GOD BLESSES

*When the great oak is straining in the wind,*
*The boughs drink in new beauty, and the trunk*
*Sends down a deeper root on the windward side.*
*Only the soul that knows the mighty grief*
*Can know the mighty rapture. Sorrows come*
*To stretch out spaces in the heart for joy.*
*—Edwin Markham*

A FEW YEARS ago the Berlin Wall fell with a shocking crash. I once saw the wall and even went through the famous Checkpoint Charlie to the other side. I remember a long, ugly blockwide strip of land that separated East and West Berlin. On that visit, I saw the barbwire, the minefields, and the tank traps designed to thwart any would-be escapist. The Berlin Wall was one tough, impenetrable wall.

The wall had been there for most of my adult life, and I never anticipated that it would come down in my lifetime. Neither did the CIA. And neither did all the other intelligence experts to whom we pay billions of dollars each year to inform us of the future. No one I know foresaw the wall's demise until the last minute.

Of course now that the wall and East Germany are no more, we can go back in recent history and see it all with better eyes. Now we know what we should have known all along: the signs pointing to the wall's imminent demise were all there. We weren't smart enough to discern them at the time. The right set of eyes might have seen it all coming. But trapped by our own points of view, we never saw what was about to happen.

The Berlin Wall is its own parable of life. Like the wall, so many lives—religious and not so religious—appear to stand strong and impenetrable. And then one day there is a fall. It comes as a disruptive moment. And then the true test of what is really strong and enduring begins.

Funny thing! In most cases you could have seen the disruptive moment coming if you'd had the right kind of foresight. But most of us do not have that natural facility to spot our own vulnerabilities. We may have eyes that see all that is beyond ourselves. But we need eyes that look into the soul.

All of the words of this book have been designed to make one simple point comparable to the Berlin Wall parable. If there isn't weight below the waterline, there will be an inevitable collapse. Man cannot live by bread alone, the Scripture says. And man cannot live without attending to his soul.

So, to use the words of one of the spiritual masters, this is why we must salute our souls: why we must acknowledge the soul's existence, its capacity to be a fountain of nobility or barbarianism.

Thus, we open the doors of our souls and go to work. We employ the greatest power in the world to first prepare the soul: *repentance.* This is the ruthless self-appraisal that leads to sorrow of soul and confession of sin. We let *the disruptive moments* provide insight and learning; we do not fight the pain, for it has a message. We give the soul *a mission,* a sense of destiny toward which it can point. *We clear it of foul motives and memories* that can serve only as a seedbed for sin. We prepare the soil of the soul by affirmation of *the great theological truths of who God is.* And we harvest the bloom of *convictions,* which translate into Christlike behavior. We engage in *prayer and intercession,* the great connection with heaven. And we pray fervently, "Come, Spirit of Jesus; dwell within and find my soul a hospitable place from which You can raise a standard of honor to God."

Not long ago, there was a conference of Christ-followers in England. At one meeting a Chinese pastor who had spent eighteen years in prison for his faith was introduced to give his witness to the assembled people. He recalled for the audience his prison experience with these words:

"My friends wonder what kind of work I did in the labor camp to keep me physically healthy. I answered them that life in the labor camp was very, very hard. The authorities in the camp put me to emptying the human waste cesspool.

"Most of the prisoners were afraid to approach the cesspool, but the authorities were aware of my background—I was well-educated, from a well-to-do family—and especially because they were atheists and they knew I was a Christian leader. So they enjoyed putting me to work in the human waste cesspool. But they did not know in those years how I enjoyed working there.

"It was more than two meters in breadth and two meters in length, filled with human waste collected from the entire camp. Once it was full, the human waste was kept until it was ripe and then dug out and sent to the field as fertilizer. Because the pit was so deep, I could not reach the bottom to empty it, so I had to walk into the disease-ridden mass and scoop out the successive layers of human waste, all the time breathing the strong stench.

"The guards and all the prisoners kept a long way off because of the stench.

"So why did I enjoy working in the cesspool? I enjoyed the solitude. In the labor camp all the prisoners normally were under strict surveillance and no one could be alone. But when I worked in the cesspool, I could be alone and could pray to our Lord as loudly as I needed. I could recite the Scriptures including all the Psalms I still remembered and no one was close enough to protest. That's the reason I enjoyed working in the cesspool. Also I could sing loudly the hymns I still remembered.

"In those days one of my most favorite was 'In the Garden.' Before I was arrested this was my favorite hymn, but at that time I did not realize the real meaning of this hymn. When I worked in the cesspool, I knew and discovered a wonderful fellowship with our Lord. Again and again I sang this hymn and felt our Lord's presence with me.

> I come to the garden alone
> While the dew is still on the roses;
> And the voice I hear falling on my ear,
> The Son of God discloses.
> And he walks with me, and he talks with me,
> And he tells me I am his own,
> And the joy we share as we tarry there
> None other has ever known.

"Again and again as I sang this hymn in the cesspool, I experienced the Lord's presence. He never left me or forsook me. And so I survived and the cesspool became my private garden."

These are the words of a simple man whose life God has chosen to bless.

# A PARABLE

ONCE A WISE man prepared to build a boat. His intention was that his boat would provide opportunities for his family's recreation. But he also had in mind that it might be used for the enjoyment of others who could not afford to have a boat. If there were times, he thought, when he could welcome less advantaged people aboard his boat after it was built, he would be glad.

As the wise man planned for the day when the building would commence, he sat down with sailors with much more experience than himself. "What have you learned about boats?" he asked each one. "What does a good boat look like? What have been your good and bad experiences? What should I avoid? What advice do you have about what is important in the building of a boat?" And as the old sailors with their accumulated experiences spoke, he listened carefully.

They spoke to him of seas that were both beautiful and dangerous. Of islands he might someday visit. But they also spoke of shoals and sandbars to avoid. They told of the beautiful seasons for sailing and warned of sudden storms at other times. And when they got to the subject of boats, they emphasized the importance of well-designed keels and properly distributed weight below the waterline. There was talk of the shape of the kind of hull that would best cut through the water and of materials that would guarantee the seaworthiness of the boat in the roughest of times.

When he asked about sails and rigging, about cabins and fittings, they cautioned him to be practical. "Don't worry half as much about the appearance of your boat, about those things that win nautical beauty contests. Concern yourself most about materials and designs that can withstand rough waters and brutal storms. Go for sails that will not tear, masts that will not easily topple, rigging that is designed for maximum stress. Don't make your cabin a castle; make it a safe place where you can be warm and dry when the seas are rough." And so as the advice from the old sailors poured in, he recorded every comment in his notebooks.

The picture of a strong sailboat began to emerge on the architect's table. With every passing day, it became clear: this boat would provide maximum enjoyment for a wise man, his family, and his friends. It would offer safety and stability. "Why," some said, "this is the kind of boat you'd feel confident sailing to Europe or around the world."

Only when the plans were complete did the wise man begin to build. And as he'd been advised, he gave careful attention to those parts of the boat that no one would ever see once the boat was put into the water. Yes, there were moments of temptation to get more quickly to the more visible aspects of the boat. But when the temptations came, so also did the memory of the horror stories and the counsel of the older sailors. And he returned to what he'd learned was most important.

Thus, the keel was laid; the hull was carefully built. And upon that foundation the remainder of the boat was built. The old sailors often stopped by with words of encouragement and counsel. And each time they came, there were enthusiastic conversation and rich assurance. The wise man was on the right track, they said.

But other members of the boat club took little or no notice. They preferred their cocktails, the club dances, the Sunday afternoon regattas with all the clubbiness that went along with such life. When they spoke of boats in the harbor, they spoke of color and brand names and expensive gadgets. But they spoke hardly at all about the wise man's craft, which was slowly being built at one end of the club's wharf. It was all too obvious: they weren't impressed, and they weren't interested.

On the day the boat that the wise man had built was finished, he arranged for it to be lowered into the water. His family was there, and the old sailors joined them. And they cheered as he pointed the boat toward the harbor's entrance for its maiden voyage. As the sailing craft turned its bow toward the sea, all those who were watching noticed the name the wise man had painted on the stern: the *Christos*. Some knew the significance of the name; but others did not, and they wondered.

It was a beautiful day when the wise man pointed the *Christos* out to sea. Across the horizon were a thousand boats, so it seemed, each bobbing along as the gentle rhythms of the waves moved them about. The sun was high and the breeze was moderate. It was, all in all, a magnificent day for sailing.

A magnificent day, that was, until midafternoon. And then suddenly a storm from seemingly nowhere swept in. There was hardly a warning! The Coast Guard had not predicted a storm, and it caught everyone as a terrible surprise. Suddenly, boats were no longer gently bobbing up and down. They were pitching and tossing. Soon everyone was headed at full power toward the harbor, but the wind made it difficult to make headway. In a few minutes the radio waves were filled with distress calls: Mayday! Mayday! Here and there one could see any number of boats lying on their sides, their owners climbing on to inflatable rafts and hoping for rescue.

The wise man in his new boat, the *Christos*, saw all of this. He could feel his newly built craft responding to the storm. Each wave that fell across the decks was a test of the boat's strength. But the wise man had built a strong yacht. The weight below the waterline kept it steady on course, and while the stiffest of wind gusts often blew the boat over to one side or the other, it always righted itself as sailboats were designed to do. Before long the wise man was filled with confidence that if he was diligent with his skills and strength, he could ride out the storm.

But riding out the storm was not enough. He also set forth to attempt the rescue of others whose boats were not built for such tempests. As the winds blew and the waves mounted with greater force, the wise man steered his boat in one direction and then another plucking hapless sailors from the sea. And only when the *Christos* was low in the water because of the weight of so many sailors pulled from the ocean did the wise man turn toward the harbor and for the safety of its calm waters.

Today in the front entrance of the club's restaurant, there is a large painting on the wall. Everyone who enters sees this first of all. The wise man stands in the foreground of this painting, and behind him is the *Christos*. Beneath the painting is a statement of commendation written and signed by the members of the boat club. It recalls the heroic efforts of the wise man and the incredible resiliency of his remarkable boat on the day of the great storm. When you look at this painting and you read the commendation, you know one thing for sure: this wise man will never be forgotten.

# B I B L I O G R A P H Y

Alsop, Joseph W. *I've Seen the Best of It: The Memoirs of Joseph W. Alsop.* New York: Norton, 1992.

Begbie, Harold. *The Life of General William Booth.* New York: Macmillan, 1920.

Bloom, Anthony. *Beginning to Pray.* Mahwah, N.J.: Paulist Press, 1982.

Buechner, Frederick. *Telling Secrets.* New York: HarperCollins, 1991.

Chambers, Whittiker. *Witness.* New York: Random House, 1952.

Chesterton, G. K. *St. Francis of Assisi.* New York: Doubleday, 1987.

Hall, Clarence. *Portrait of a Prophet: The Biography of Samuel Logan Brengle.* New York: Salvation Army Supply House Depot, 1933.

Herman, E. *Creative Prayer.* Santa Fe: Sun Pub, 1993.

Heschel, Abraham Joshua. *The Earth Is the Lord's.* New York: Harper Torchbooks, 1966.

*The Sabbath.* New York: Harper Torchbooks, 1966.

Jones, E. S. *The Unshakable Kingdom and the Unchanging Person.* Nashville: Abingdon Press, 1972.

Kelley, Thomas. *A Testament of Devotion.* New York: Harper, 1941.

Moody, William R. *The Life of Dwight L. Moody.* Tarrytown, N.J.: Revell, 1900.

Pibworth, Nigel R. *The Gospel Pedlar: John Berridge & the 18th Century Revival.* Welwyn, England: Evangelical Press, 1987.

Robinson, Edwin Arlington. "Richard Corey." In *American Poetry and*

*Prose,* edited by Norman Foster et al. Boston: Houghton Mifflin, 1947.

Shoemaker, Samuel. "I Stand by the Door." In *I Stand by the Door* by Helen S. Shoemaker. New York: Harper, 1967.

Wheeler, W. Reginald. *A Man Sent from God: The Life of Robert Speer.* Tarrytown, N.J.: Revell, 1956.

Wilbur, Richard. "Parable." In *Oxford Book of Short Poems*, edited by James Michie and P. J. Kavanagh. New York: Oxford University Press, 1985.

Yeats, William Butler. *Book of Religious Verse.* New York: Oxford University Press, 1972.

### Preface: The Life God Blesses and The *Persona*: A Parable

1. What have you believed is the origin of the soul? Is your belief grounded in Scripture, or is it an opinion? Read Genesis 2:7 and 1 Corinthians 15:44–46.

2. Where in you does your soul reside? Does it matter?

3. Is it possible for people to be soulless? If so, what sort of persons are they?

4. What is the message behind the parable of the foolish boat builder?

### Chapter 1: Lost at Sea

1. What does the author mean when he refers to things "below the waterline"?

2. Is the weight of your life above or below your personal water-line? Compare where the balance is in your life to how a sailboat must be balanced.

3. What happens to a sailboat if too much weight is above the waterline? Make a mental leap from sailboat design to lifestyle design. Is yours top-heavy or about right?

4. Make a list of any areas of your life that could be off balance. How can you return to an even keel?

## Chapter 2: Storms Happen

1. When one of life's storms hits you, do you pray to God about it or blame Him for it? Enlist the prayers of friends to help you overcome a life-storm.

2. Have you waited until catastrophe struck before asking the right questions? Focus on one of your life-storms, past or present. What, if anything, could you have done to lessen its effects?

3. If you define the workings of the soul with inadequate words, are you limiting the size of the soul? How does the author say the soul should be measured?

4. What is a spiritual master? Name at least two that you know, or know about.

5. Isn't a "spiritual waterline" actually a way of discerning the visible from the invisible in our lives? Which part of our lives, visible or invisible, consumes most of our thinking? Give reasons for why it is that way.

6. Draw a long horizontal line on a piece of paper. The line is your personal spiritual waterline. Write down all the things in your life that you feel are above the waterline and all the things that are below it.

## Chapter 3: Storms and Disruptive Moments

1. Would you describe your adulthood as zooming down the interstate highway of life or as being full of detours and jolts from potholes? Explain why you chose your answer.

2. Can you recall the first major disruptive event in your life? What was its effect on you? How did your attitudes or beliefs change as a result of it?

3. Do you agree with the premise that the only way to learn what life is truly about comes through suffering? What is the basis for your opinion?

4. Make a statement summarizing what a disruptive moment is and why these moments are significant.

5. Why are disruptive moments the prelude for soul-talk?

6. The author describes four major kinds of disruptive moments: crisis, wonderment, aging, and spiritual discipline. What are the distinctive characteristics of each type? Is there a common purpose for all of them?

7. Of the four disruptive moments, what is the only one under your control?

## Chapter 4: Quality of Soul

1. What is meant by the quality of a soul?

2. If you are living out of the soul, what are you doing?

3. Have you been seeking *spirituality* or a *spiritual experience?* Explain the difference.

4. Why would a person mistake a spiritual experience for spirituality?

5. Give an example of a spiritual experience you have had. What were the circumstances? Did the effects on you cause a permanent change in your life, or did you soon get back to "life as usual"?

6. What is the likely consequence to the faith of someone who has a failed spiritual experience?

7. Does every spiritual experience have a temporary effect? Can a spiritual experience lead to deeper spirituality? How?

## Chapter 5: Questing for Spirituality

1. Cite an example of spirituality in a person you know.

2. Note your ideas about how a person with spirituality deals differently with life's problems from someone without it.

3. Why is youth rarely found among the ranks of those possessing great spirituality?

4. Have you set aside some time each week to be completely silent and alone so you may submit yourself to learning God's Word? If not, choose a good time for you, right now, and stick to it.

5. What will be the greatest benefit for you in doing this?

6. When was the last time you sat down and read, or thought about something, in complete silence? That means no TV, no radio, no other people around. Just you and complete silence. Have those times slipped away from you? What can you do to bring them back?

7. Why is silence good for the soul?

8. Read Psalm 46:10 and hold to its advice.

## Chapter 6: The Stare of the Snake

1. What are the only two sources of evil?

2. Identify the scriptural basis for the snake as the embodiment of evil.

3. Do you believe that evil is the result of external forces working upon us, or does it emanate from rottenness inside us? Read Matthew 15:19–20 and substitute the word *soul* for the word *heart*.

4. Have you always believed that people are basically good? Why is this commonly held view at odds with what the Scriptures

tell us? How do you rationalize a position that is not scripturally based?

5. What is a "road to Damascus experience"? What is its origin?

6. Describe in your words the stare of the snake. How can you break the stare?

## Chapter 7: What Kind of an Old Man Do You Want to Be?

1. If we are to live out of the soul, what must we do?

2. Will the realization that you are getting older be a disruptive moment for you? Explain your answer.

3. Answer the question: What kind of an old man do you want to be? Make a list. Were most of the things on your list spiritual or earthly? Why?

4. What should your emphasis be for question 3? If you are under fifty, why bother thinking about what kind of old man you want to be?

5. What is the first mark (or sign) of a decadent culture? See Romans 1:21–23.

6. Define *macro-thinking*. Describe how your thinking process compares to your definition of macro-thinking.

7. Do great men and women tend to be macro-thinkers? Why or why not?

8. Explain why a grandparent often handles a situation so much differently from the way a parent does.

9. What is your perspective on death? What is meant by "everyone wants to go to heaven, but no one wants to die"?

## Chapter 8: A Soul Shaped by Mission

1. Describe in simple terms why you exist and what purpose you are serving.

2. Do you and your spouse have a shared sense of mission for your family? Try writing it down.

3. Does the soul need a sense of direction, or is it innate? If you think that it needs direction, where does direction come from?

4. Name the five items a mission statement might include.

5. Write down a mission statement for the rest of your life. Make periodic updates, and read it often.

6. Repeat to yourself the mission statement of Jesus. See Luke 19:9–10.

7. Do you face an overabundance of choices in your life? Which ones can you do without? Which should you keep?

8. As best you can and in your own words, try to describe the mission statements of Winston Churchill, Martin Luther King, Jr., and Billy Graham.

9. What is the mission of all creation? Explain.

## Chapter 9: A Beautiful Soul

1. Is the term *a beautiful soul* just a euphemism for a nice person? Explain what a beautiful soul means to you.

2. What is the soul meant to be?

3. Define *repentance*. What does repenting do for your soul and your life?

4. Have you tried to please God or people in your life? Is it possible to please both? Read Matthew 6:24.

5. Reread the five thought-provoking questions the author explains in this chapter. Write them down and answer each one honestly.

6. The soul can begin its pilgrimage toward beauty only if what happens?

## Chapter 10: Where Will You Be?

1. Where will you be spiritually when God calls you? Read Luke 12:20 for understanding and urgency.

2. If you have quiet times to commune with God, is asking or praising more typical? Which is more likely to grow your soul?

3. Repeat the author's definition of *theology*. Then come up with your own definition.

4. Is all creativity meant to reflect the glory and honor of the Creator? The author says yes. Express your opinion on this topic.

5. Make a statement showing how humans' creations (art, music, literature, etc.) and God's creations differ.

6. Is there a final accountability for us? Read about the white throne judgment in Revelation 20:11–13.

7. Explain the gift of redemption.

8. List some ways in which God shows He is a Father with compassion and intimacy for His children.

9. Draw up a list with the names of people who are in heaven now, and why you would like to talk with them when you get there (for example, a relative, a friend, a historical figure, or a biblical leader).

## Chapter 11: Convictions Grow in Special Soil

1. The soul is the ideal growing place for _____, which could also be called _____.

2. The product of the mind is rationality and logic. Compare this with the definition of faith in Hebrews 11:1.

3. Explain the difference between convictions and feelings.

4. If convictions drive performance, what do feelings do?

5. The author says to describe someone as having a character flaw is not correct because all character is flawed. What does he mean?

6. Name the sources of our convictions, and give a brief description of each.

7. Have you experienced a major failure in your life (for example, business failure, bankruptcy, divorce)? Express how a major failure forced the development of new convictions in your life.

8. What is the one thing that is worse than a failure?

9. How can we rebuild a character that has slipped from good standing?

10. Make a list of the goals and objectives you believe the Lord has set for your life.

## Chapter 12: I Call It Soul-Talk

1. Just what is soul-talk?

2. What could be an undesirable side effect of too much aloneness?

3. What is the most proper environment for soul-talk?

4 The ability to wait is called patience. What role does it play in praying and looking for results?

5. What restrictions, conditions, or time frames should we put on and in our prayers? Why?

## Chapter 13: Where Does the Energy Come From?

1. What is the power that turns common people into exceptional citizens in the kingdom of God?

2. Are the workings of the Holy Spirit available to only a few? To only the original apostles? Will the Holy Spirit work through you? Read Luke 11:13 and Acts 2:38; 10:44.

3. If the family spirit conveys the honor of the family, what does the Holy Spirit convey to human beings?

4. Explain the fruit of the Holy Spirit. When do we receive the fruit of the Holy Spirit?

5. What is the purpose of the gifts of the Holy Spirit?

6. Read 1 Corinthians 12:7–14. Have you ever experienced any of these gifts? What must you do to receive them?

7. Why do human beings need the power of the Holy Spirit?

8. Complete this sentence. "If I wanted to bring the power of the Holy Spirit into my life, I would . . ."

9. The next time you pray with a group, ask the Holy Spirit to enter the lives of those willing to receive Him.

**Gordon MacDonald** is senior pastor of Grace Chapel in Lexington, Massachusetts, and is the author of more than ten books, including *Rebuilding Your Broken World* and *Christ Followers in the Real World*. He is a frequent speaker at conferences, men's and pastors' seminars, and lay renewal convocations. Gordon and his wife, Gail, travel internationally, speaking to churches and missionaries.

Gordon MacDonald's best-loved works can now be found in **The Gordon MacDonald Bestseller Series**, each including a study guide for individual or group use. Look for the following other titles in the series:

### Renewing Your Spiritual Passion

Gordon MacDonald shares many personal experiences with readers to pinpoint various problem areas that relate to spiritual exhaustion and mental fatigue. With this book, he helps readers recognize the areas of spiritual deficit and its causes and provides solutions for rekindling their passion for God.

**0-7852-7162-7 • Trade Paperback • $12.99 • 240 pages**

### When Men Think Private Thoughts

MacDonald addresses the questions men often ask of themselves, exploring avenues that include sexuality and masculinity; intimacy, romance, and friendship; and achievement and definitions of success, revealing how each road intersects with a man's soul. Readers will be able to put aside the stereotypical definitions of maleness that plague men's private thoughts and will see instead a Christ-centered model. This book was designed for men, but will also help women better understand the men they love.

**0-7852-7163-5 • Trade Paperback • $12.99 • 288 pages**

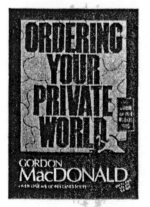

### Ordering Your Private World

This bestseller has already helped over a million readers find a sense of being satisfied from the inside out. By working through five specific areas—motivation, use of time, wisdom and knowledge, spiritual strength, and restoration—MacDonald gives readers helpful advice for fighting the disorder within and experiencing personal growth and spiritual development.

**0-7852-7161-9 • Trade Paperback • $12.99 • 228 pages**